PRAISE FOR *THE FINDERS*

"If a Nobel Prize existed for Psychology, the work done by Jeffery Martin and his team and described in this book would be a strong contender. The book is about people who have managed to fulfill one of the most sought after but rarely achieved human needs—true happiness, a deep and fundamental sense of wellbeing."

~ Dr. Peter Fenwick, internationally renowned neuropsychiatrist and Fellow of the Royal College of Psychiatrists

"Dr. Jeffery Martin's work on non-symbolic states of awareness has helped create the most lucid map for understanding higher states of consciousness. I have personally gained a deeper understanding of the universality of human sacred experience from his research and have been able to replicate and publish it. For anyone who is interested in getting scientific knowledge of the range and evolution of human experience in the direction of expanded awareness and ultimately that which wisdom traditions call 'enlightenment' Jeffery's book and research are must reads."

~ Deepak Chopra, MD, FACP, founder of The Chopra Foundation and co-founder of The Chopra Center for Wellbeing, author of over 85 books including dozens of best sellers

"In this book Dr. Martin takes his place beside William James and Abraham Maslow to give us one of the most important and ground-breaking works on consciousness and human potential in recent memory."

~ Allan Leslie Combs, Ph.D., CIIS Professor of Consciousness Studies, author of *The Radiance of Being* and *Consciousness Explained Better*

"In *The Finders*, Dr. Martin has made a real contribution. First he's defined a whole new class of folks' experiences: the enlightened, the *illuminati*, the deeply fulfilled, which is oft discussed and little understood. So, a careful and traditional transcending study of it is long overdue. While we've heard of these folks, by looking carefully at their experiences, he's been able to categorize their experiences, with clear, albeit complex and flexible, categories. To do so his interviews were thorough and have led to intelligible analyzes. This is a decade-long project and well worth his time and our study. An important book!"

~ Robert K.C. Forman, Ph.D., D.Hon., founding editor of the *Journal of Consciousness Studies*, author of *Enlightenment Ain't What It's Cracked Up To Be*

But who is to determine what is genuine? Science endeavors to do so regarding everything external instruments can measure but has generally dismissed the experiences of mystics as fancies unworthy of their attention.

Can subjective states be scrutinized empirically? Are people experiencing these states more fully aligning with nature's intelligence? If so, could sufficient numbers of them transform our culture and our technologies and reverse the destructive trends that threaten us all?

Jeffery Martin has made and continues to make a significant contribution to answering these questions, and in the process, enabling others to answer them for themselves. He is bridging the unnecessary and unproductive gulf between science and spirituality and devising practical applications for his research as it unfolds. I think his work is among the most significant taking place on the planet today."

~ Rick Archer, Co-Producer and Host, Buddha at the Gas Pump podcast, which has interviewed hundreds of Finders (https://batgap.com)

"*The Finders* is a fascinating description of the ways in which people can find their greatest sense of well-being. The research is fundamental to understanding how experiences of fundamental wellbeing occur and provides new insights that will propel ongoing investigations. Essential for anyone striving for this type of well-being."

~ Andrew Newberg, M.D., Professor and Director of Research for the Marcus Institute of Integrative Health at Thomas Jefferson University, author of *How Enlightenment Changes Your Brain*

"Dr. Jeffery A. Martin has written a highly readable, enlightening account of his groundbreaking research into the Fundamental Wellbeing. His Finders Course is among the most universally accessible methods for introducing one to nonduality to emerge in years. It can help one with the initial and perhaps the most difficult step in realizing nonduality, that of experiencing oneself free of the incessant subconscious gossip of one's narrative self. His work contributes to the ongoing transformation of human society from the fear driven egoism, nationalism and prejudice, into the global culture of compassion, wisdom and happiness."

~ Zoran Josipovic, PhD, leading neuroscience of consciousness researcher, adjunct Assistant Professor for Cognitive and Affective Neuroscience at New York University

"Dr. Jeffery Martin's work on Persistent Non-Symbolic Experience is among the most promising recent developments in contemporary consciousness research and I am thrilled that it is beginning to see the light of day. Both coherent with age-old wisdom yet also stretching prevailing boundaries and assumptions about the manifestation of these developmental stages, Fundamental Wellbeing needs to be an essential component in any 21st century consciousness studies curricular or research program. I look forward to incorporating it in my own work."

– Ed Sarath, Professor of Music and Director of the Program in Creativity and Consciousness Studies, at the University of Michigan; author of *Improvisation, Creativity and Consciousness*, and *Black Music Matters*

"*The Finders* is a riveting, ambitious and fun account by Dr. Jeffery A. Martin of some basic realities in our world, that human beings are seeking what he terms Fundamental Wellbeing and fulfillment, beyond labels, philosophical leanings and what many claim a unique spirituality that they possess. Jeffery has carried out a lot of work and in his book provides fascinating details that will appeal to many, even to their own surprise when they find out that what they are seeking is commonly sought out by many others. I highly recommend it for those of us who feel that there is something common in all of us, yet that our own uniqueness should be honored and celebrated."

– Menas C. Kafatos, PhD, Fletcher Jones Endowed Professor of Computational Physics at Chapman University, and author of *The Conscious Universe* and *You Are The Universe*

"It is a rare find to see a rigorous and well-designed, global longitudinal study of the transpersonal territory of human experience. This one explores the people called Finders, the folks who are inherently happy no matter what the circumstances. The report is written in a lucid, caring and accessible style. It never claims insights that have not been validated as of yet. Moreover, it introduces several novel and crucial distinctions and clarifications in the field of ongoing non-symbolic experiences and lasting, profound wellbeing.

Are you a Seeker or a Finder, for instance, and how can one tell? Where are the Finders and what makes them different from most people who struggle to navigate life. Are there levels of "finding?" How come we get so attached to our Narrative-Self and what is life like free of stories?

This is a must read for all those who explore the transpersonal field from whatever perspective, including any spiritual or religious leaning as well as atheist and agnostics. Dr. Martin's overall thesis challenges much received knowledge and many widely-shared assumptions about how to "achieve" lasting contentment.

It is also a life-affirming read for those skeptical of any belief system no matter how ancient. We, too, can become Finders as faith in some higher being or post-death salvation is not a requirement. The study shows that benevolence and total inner calm can be found in people across the globe and in all walks of life."

~ Dr. Susanne Cook-Greuter, internationally renowned authority
on adult development; author of *Creativity, Spirituality, and
Transcendence: Paths to Integrity and Wisdom in the Mature Self*,
and *Transcendence and Mature Thought in Adulthood*; creator
of the term "non-symbolically mediated consciousness."

"This easily readable, yet profound, book is based on in-depth interviews of people who have managed to see through their "narrative" selves, the made-up drama which gives a sense of coherency but also too often is mistaken for the actual living person experiencing much more than any mere story could ever tell. Those free from the limitations of believing that their own narrative is all they are, including free from the all too often incessant-inner clamor that continually constructs and reinforces their personal stories, along with the concomitant suffering attached to these stories, are labeled as "Finders" for having seen through this fundamental delusion endemic within the modern world. They are, instead, enabled to experience the suchness of themselves and the world more directly without the clouding of words. Freedom from being encapsulated in such isolating-individualistic self-stories, however, does not always come without cost—and this book courageously faces both the upsides and downsides of finding oneself one with verbally unmediated experience of what is. Reminiscent of Alan Watts' *The Book on the Taboo Against Knowing Who You Are*, but speaking to a new generation and grounded in people's actual experiences, this book provides a useful guide for those seeking, as well as those already living in ways congruent with, such radical freedom and its related responsibility."

~ Harris L. Friedman, PhD, Co-President of the Association for
Transpersonal Psychology; Research Professor of Psychology, University of
Florida; co-editor of *The Handbook of Transpersonal Psychology*

The Finders

Dr. Jeffery A. Martin

THE FINDERS

Integration Press
P.O. Box 8906
Jackson, Wyoming 83002

Hardcover ISBN: 1-57242-555-5

ISBN13: 978-1-57242-555-2

Paperback ISBN: 1572425563

ISBN 13: 978-1-57242-556-9

Library of Congress Control Number: 2018913226

Printed in the United States of America.

Cover designed by: Cathi Stevenson

Interior designed by: Gwen Gades

Edited by: Rod Pennington, Emily Han, Mark Antonides

Dedicated to all of the research participants around the world who generously gave of their time so that this project could happen, the researchers and collaborators who also made it possible, and to Finders everywhere.

CONTENTS

PREFACE

At the turn of the new century, I was the classic overachiever with a flourishing career and amazing relationships with my family and friends. Despite this, I wasn't all that happy. So, I decided to drop everything, go on a quest to find the happiest people on Earth, study them, and see if I could figure out how to join their ranks. As crazy as this sounds, it actually worked.

The segment of the general population that rose to the top are often considered spiritual or religious. They refer to themselves as "enlightened," "nondual," "persistently mystical," experiencing the "peace that passeth understanding," and by hundreds of similar descriptions. I went on to learn that many atheists and agnostics also experience similar levels of wellbeing, and that the religious or spiritual components are optional. Some of these individuals had just stumbled into these further reaches of wellbeing and weren't even sure how they'd arrived, but many were active seekers who had become *Finders*.

For over a decade now, these individuals have welcomed me into their homes and lives. In fact, over these past years most of my time has been spent researching and learning from them. Thousands have passed through the project in one way or another. Eventually, I learned enough to both join them and help others do the same.

As the years progressed and the data from this massive, first-ever, global academic research project piled up, it became increasingly clear that we had much to offer them as well. No one had previously reached out to collect their information, or study them, like our project had. Despite its profundity, the significant internal change that accompanies the shift that we call *Fundamental Wellbeing* in this book, and *Ongoing* or *Persistent Non-Symbolic Experience* (*ONE/PNSE*) academically, is largely a mystery, even to those who experience it. In fact, the Finders themselves are often curious about it. How prevalent is it? How do others experience it? How have others found ways to optimize certain aspects of it? Is there a known landscape involving it? What can *really* be done with it?

Our project collected the first broad snapshot of answers to questions like these. Accordingly, it seemed important that our first major publication based on this research should be in service to the remarkable community of individuals worldwide that made it all possible. So, this book is mostly written for and to all of them, with our deep gratitude and thanks.

This is a dense and information-packed book that drills to the core of our research. I resisted the urge, and editors' attempts, to lighten it up because I wanted to ensure that everything possible was put into it. I hope you find it helpful. It's designed to provide a comprehensive description of these types of human experience.

As the book unfolded, it was clear that a second audience would also be attracted to and could benefit from it. Hundreds of thousands of people, possibly more, around the world are devoting their lives to trying to reach Fundamental Wellbeing. I hear from them all the time. They are often reaching out in desperation, having tried many paths that never led to their goal. Our research puts us in a unique situation to serve this population of seekers, so they are included here as well.

If you already experience Fundamental Wellbeing, you can feel free to skip the first few chapters. They have been written to provide some additional context for seekers. You'll notice that these chapters have a slightly different, more personal voice. They also provide some background information that isn't needed once you've gone from seeker to Finder.

Although the first public draft of this book is being released in 2019, it has existed in many forms since 2010. Hundreds of both seekers and Finders read and commented on the manuscript, and helped to shape it over time into its current form. It's common for authors to publish a series of works over the years as their understanding evolves. I find that this can be confusing for people in later time periods, when many revisions of the work exist, and I didn't want to follow this path. Instead, I chose to wait until we had maximum confidence in the data being presented here and it seemed unlikely that it would need to undergo significant later revisions.

Over time, and countless drafts, I've learned that it is impossible to please all readers. A tiny handful want the scientific stats and data, seekers often want stories that engage their minds, and Finders typically want neither of these. Here are a few of the key decisions I've made that have led to the most feedback, both positive and negative, depending upon the group. I want to address them up front so you don't get hung up on them as you read, and can understand why I'm presenting things the way I am.

First of all, the transition to Fundamental Wellbeing generally reduces the desire for stories. Because this book is written primarily for Finders, I've kept this in mind. Stories are also often used to simplify, and thus can hide complexity. I wanted this book to be as thorough a representation of our data as possible, so when I've included stories, it is because I felt they represent most or all of the point needing to be made.

In earlier drafts, when a story was used, seekers who read the book would often take the example it provided as the penultimate case for what was being discussed. In fact, there were probably dozens to hundreds of other, different stories and examples that would have provided alternative perspectives around the same point. Therefore, I've actively sought to minimize this type of confusion and incorporate straightforward writing instead.

Because it was written for Western, English speakers, I've slightly tilted many of the religious and spiritual examples towards Christianity and away from Eastern religions like Buddhism and Hinduism. A number of seekers who read the draft were familiar with or practiced one of the latter, and commented on this over the years. I've done this simply because the vast majority of readers are likely to have the Christian tradition somewhere in their background, and I've learned that this provides useful common ground for most readers. At the same time, I've worked hard to also incorporate examples from a range of various traditions, all of which we encountered during the project.

A couple of notes regarding punctuation: I have used double quotes (" ") in a specific way to allow the research participants' voices to shine through in the text. Sometimes these encase a word-for-word quote from a participant; however, more often they denote a commonly used term or paraphrased concept that the participants used while discussing a given topic. Single quotes (' ') are most often used to provide a characterization or coloration that is my own.

You may also notice that I've chosen to use the rarer, non-hyphenated form of the word *wellbeing*. This was not an accident. I simply think it reads better when used so many times. For the first couple of years I used the standard form in the book, but many people's eyes seem to trip up on it. Rather than use it less or adopt a less appropriately descriptive term, I simply adopted this form.

A final note: When the first draft of this book was finished eight years ago, it was originally intended for both academics and individuals who experienced Fundamental Wellbeing. Over seemingly endless drafts and rounds of feedback, it became clear that the needs of these audiences were too different for a single book. The statistics and other in-depth research data the earlier drafts contained seemed to ensure that only academics would wade through it. While my scholarly friends have been asking for a comprehensive write up of this data for a long time, I hope they will forgive me for ultimately deciding to serve my research population first. Anyone wanting to see the data can find it at the Center for the Study of Non-Symbolic Consciousness website:

nonsymbolic.org

Much Love,
Jeffery

INTRODUCTION

The average person lives with an experience of the world that is rooted in fear, worry, anxiety, and scarcity. Perhaps the most common way this manifests is in a persistent sense of discontentment. *Something* just doesn't feel quite right.

That something is usually hard to put a finger on. It's often just a feeling that haunts us in the background, one that leads to endless soul searching and goal striving. Although it can disappear when a desire is achieved, or a piece of our life that was believed to be missing falls into place, ultimately the relief is only temporary. Before long, the background feeling that something is not okay returns and the search begins anew.

You may be surprised to learn that life doesn't have to be this way. Since 2006, our global scientific research project has been on the trail of the tiny fraction of the population that seems to have escaped this fate. We found thousands of them, and what we learned has been nothing short of astonishing. It will revolutionize your life for the better, if you'll let it.

Imagine having your discontent and fear replaced by a sense that everything is fundamentally okay, that you are safe, whole, and fine just as you are. This does not mean that you can't function effectively in the world. If someone points a gun at you, you'll respond appropriately. However, your mind will no longer spend all day worrying about whether you are good enough, what might be a threat to you, how the world views you, or any of the other thoughts that, ultimately, aren't serving you.

Simply put, you'll be at peace and able to thrive and enjoy life.

DR. ABRAHAM MASLOW'S SECRET

One of the world's leading psychologists, Dr. Abraham Maslow is known for his famous pyramid representing the hierarchy of human needs, with its base formed from physiological needs and *self-*

actualization at the apex. The general idea is that we must have our basic needs, like food, met before all others. Then we must have our safety needs met. Then we need to be loved and respected. When all of that is in place, we can finally be self-actualized.

Self-actualization can be defined as "the achievement of one's full potential through creativity, independence, spontaneity, and a grasp of the real world" (dictionary.com) or "the desire for self-fulfillment… the tendency…to become actualized in what…[you are]…potentially" (Maslow, *A Theory of Human Motivation*). It's essentially meant to represent how far you can develop as an individual in the world.

Let me ask you a question.

Have you made it? Are you self-actualized? Have you reached this pinnacle of human experience?

If you're like most people, you probably feel that you have, at least to some extent.

But, did you know that towards the end of his life Maslow altered his famous theory? Essentially, this revision made self-actualization second place in terms of what is possible to experience as a human. Very few people have learned about his important final masterstroke, and for good reason.

In the late 1960's, Maslow was very sick from a heart condition, and he died in June 1970 before his final modification could be widely disseminated. However, he did find the time to form an entirely new category of psychology around it. He called it Transpersonal Psychology.

Why this name?

The highest level in the final form of Maslow's work is *self-transcendence*. You can think of it as transcending the limitations of the individual self, and tapping into the resources of something that's beyond it. That may sound a little strange, but keep in mind that Maslow was a highly rigorous and respected scientist. In fact, during this same period he was president of the leading academic organization for psychologists, the highly-prestigious American Psychological Association. When he referred to self-transcendence, he was talking about highly specific psychological phenomena.

Most humans spend their entire lives trying to self-actualize by building up and refining their ego, or individualized sense of self. Far from who and what they actually are, what Maslow discovered is that the ego is actually just a tiny part of what makes someone up. In subsequent years, the fields of psychology, cognitive science, and neuroscience all affirmed this perspective. We now know that even just the conscious part of our experience is but a tiny fraction of overall brain activity. Imagine how much smaller the part of this is that relates to just the ego? There's simply no way it could be the totality of who we actually are.

Towards the end of his life, Maslow was adamant that it was best not to get caught up in the self-actualized level, just as one doesn't want to get hung up on something lower in his pyramid, like food or love. For example, an individual can easily center their life on the 'Love and Belonging' level, which includes things like family, friendship, and sexual intimacy. This can lead to a perfectly fine life, but not maxing this level out and rising above it also makes it a limiting prison. Accordingly, self-actualization will also confine you to experience less than you otherwise can if you don't rise above it. It's an amazing level for a human to reach, but Maslow tells us there's a better one—self-transcendence. Going beyond the ego; beyond the individual sense of self.

Maslow experienced this highest level himself near the very end of his life and called it the *high-plateau experience*. We refer to it academically as Ongoing or Persistent forms of Non-Symbolic Experience (ONE or PNSE), and in this book we call it Fundamental Wellbeing.

In many ways, our work picked up thirty-five years later from where Maslow's unfortunate passing left off.

WHAT MAKES FUNDAMENTAL WELLBEING SO GREAT?

Religions, spiritual systems, philosophies, and mythologies have carried the knowledge of Fundamental Wellbeing forward for millennia, across the rise and fall of empires. Today, our project and others are exploring it with science. Psychology is used to examine its effects on personality and people's moment-to-moment experience.

Neuroscience is probing the brain, and biology the body, uncovering what is unique about the individuals who experience it, and what sets them apart from everyone else. At this point, we've spent over a decade researching this. You can see a great deal about our academic research at: **nonsymbolic.org**

We've learned that there are many different forms of Fundamental Wellbeing, in large part because various cultures have not all emphasized the same aspects of it. One size does not fit all. A form that is appropriate for one person may not be for their neighbor. However, frankly, all of them are great.

In the pages that follow, you will learn about the people who have moved past their moments of doubt and frustration. They have found exactly what everyone else has been seeking their entire life. For them, each moment feels perfectly okay at a deep and fundamental level, regardless of actual life circumstances. These individuals do not dwell on past regrets or glories, nor worries about future hopes and dreams. They live peacefully in the present, while everyone else around them seems intent on trying to escape it. They've not only found fulfillment but a deep and fundamental sense of wellbeing.

Surprisingly, you probably already know one or more of these people. Since they have no external markers, if you were taken to a cocktail party where half the room was filled with them, it's unlikely you could pick out even one. Outwardly, they seem like everyone else, but internally, the way they experience the world around them couldn't be more different. This is the story of the research project that set out to find these individuals and discover what makes them tick.

Something we learned during our research is that no matter how happy you think you are now, unless you're a Finder, there is no way for you to even begin to imagine how much better your life can be. The exciting news is that its very likely that anyone can experience it.

PART 1 – THE NARRATIVE-SELF VS. FUNDAMENTAL WELLBEING

"Very often a change of self is needed more than a change of scene."
Arthur Christopher Benson

CHAPTER 1: THE SECRET OF YOU

You know that little voice in your head? Your constant companion that comments on virtually everything you experience? It's unlikely you can remember a time that it was not there prodding and rationalizing things for you. In fact, it's probably weaving a story right now. The same kind of narrative it's been constructing for as long as you can remember. It is telling you *it* isn't just a *voice*, it's *YOU!*

As you read these words, *the voice* is following along. When you pause to think things over, or your mind drifts, *the voice* inserts itself to offer its insight. With this level of intimacy, it is easy to believe this actually is the voice of the deepest part of you. If you're like most people, you likely consider this voice to be who you really are. Your truest self.

Nothing could be further from the truth.

Since 2006, my team and I have collected data from thousands of people across six continents who have extraordinary levels of wellbeing, trying to figure out what makes them so different from everyone else. What this first of its kind global academic research project has revealed is nothing short of remarkable. Outwardly, these individuals form a true cross section of humanity. They aren't from any single culture, ethnic group, religion, or socioeconomic status. No education level, age range, or gender corrals them. They are, in every sense, a group of ordinary people who were experiencing life in an astonishingly different and more positive way than the rest of the world.

Despite their diversity, a major difference our study revealed between them and others is that they know, absolutely, that *the voice* is not who they really are. They have come to understand it as one of several interrelated aspects of their mind that combine to create a distinct lens through which the world is experienced, but by no means an optimal one. They've also discovered that this narrative form of self, the stories it spins and the often-faulty advice it offers, is only one of many possible lenses, and that some are much better than others.

Far from being a central or essential part of their lives, in our research participants this chatty, self-critical, story-based form of self, which the project refers to simply as the *Narrative-Self,* has become increasingly irrelevant and in some cases even fallen completely silent. When this happened, these individuals' perception of the world profoundly changed—for the better.

When most people who look inside themselves, down to their deepest core, they find a psychological foundation that is comprised of negative building blocks, such as fear, anger, and guilt. Although once important for our survival as a species, these negatives color everything in ways few of us can even begin to understand. Once the effects of the Narrative-Self are minimized, a huge change occurs. Subjectively, it feels like a deeper and more foundational version of the true you comes into view. Practically, it shows up as a steadier experience of wellbeing and contentment. Regardless of life circumstances, it produces a deep sense that everything is okay and that you are safe. This book will refer to this very different, and utterly remarkable, way of experiencing life as *Fundamental Wellbeing.*

The difference between this and what has been traditionally regarded as 'normal' human experience is so profound that it's possible the Narrative-Self most people regard as who they are is actually their own worst enemy. Imagine if you met someone in an elevator for the first time, and they spoke to you the same way *the voice* does. Wouldn't it be a bit like being trapped in a confined space with a pushy salesperson who knew everything about you, and seemed to delight in pushing all of your hot buttons?

Would you really want to spend time talking to someone with a seemingly endless string of advice about what you should be doing with your life? Especially one whose opinions often conflicted and whose suggested fixes often led to more problems? Would you seek out the advice of someone who told you that you've been good and deserve that decadent dessert at dinner, but then makes you feel guilty when you step on the bathroom scale the next morning?

If this voice was another person, would you consider him or her your long-lost soul mate? Someone who was integral to your success in life, who you never wanted to be apart from? Or, would you try to get away from the person as quickly as possible and hope to never cross paths again?

Perhaps worst of all, *the voice* simply will not be ignored. Its very existence seems to be built on being with you in each waking moment so it can observe and comment on your every thought, feeling, memory, and action. It's easy to understand why it seems like it actually is *you*.

The good news is that the most important thing our research revealed is that the Narrative-Self is optional and its effects on your life can be minimized. Although it may completely feel like 'you,' it isn't. Once minimized or dismissed, you can personally discover the same levels of Fundamental Wellbeing that the participants in our research study, and millions of others around the world, enjoy every day.

CHAPTER 2: NARRATIVE-SELF

No one knows for sure exactly when the Narrative-Self makes its first appearance. It may be as early as ages two or three. Psychology research suggests this is the age that life memories begin forming. If true, then it's hardly surprising that you probably remember its components like *the voice* as having always been with you, and thus confuse it with who you really are.

THE PROBLEM SOLVER

Early on, especially during our developmental years, the Narrative-Self is a valuable ally. Part of it is a very astute problem solver. For example, it helps navigate where our bodies end and the world begins, and discover what behaviors will yield desired results. In our youngest years, this problem solver encourages us to cry when hungry and smile while seeking the approval of our parents. As we mature, this early success gives the problem solver part of *the voice* credibility that makes its advice increasingly difficult to ignore, and places it at the core of who we believe we are.

The brain is powerfully driven to seek success, and avoid undesirable consequences. It craves the rewards that come with being correct. Very pleasurable chemicals are released in the brain not only when we get something right or solve a problem, but also when we believe we are heading in the correct direction.

Over time, our addiction to these chemicals grows and the problem solver develops a new tendency. The Narrative-Self becomes an increasingly aggressive problem seeker and, in some cases, a problem creator. No matter how many great things are going on, it tries hard to find and point out issues, because even just working on solving problems releases these chemicals and brings tremendous rewards. Regardless of how stellar your career, stunning your personal appearance, or wonderful your relationships, the problem seeker is hard at work locating something to complain and worry about. It does this so it can identify solutions to work towards and get its pleasure fix.

Over time, this part of you that served such a vital function early in your life begins to run amuck. It is not permitting you to rest. It's not allowing you to realize how incredible your life is, in this moment, just as it is. It's too busy seeking out its next reward by finding new problems for you to attempt to remedy. Your life is riddled with things you have pursued because the Narrative-Self convinced you of their importance, but one thing is certain, following a cycle of problem finding and attempted solving does not result in high levels of wellbeing.

Psychology researchers have a great deal of evidence for why this is so, one of which they call *hedonic adaptation.* They've learned that if you win the lottery, have a major advancement in your career, suffer a major career setback, or even become a quadriplegic—after a period of months you'll be about as happy as you were before. For most people these are prime examples of best and worst case scenarios, so why is that? One simple observation is that none of these occurrences get rid of the problem finder; they only offer it new opportunities. There's more to the story, of course, and for that we need to meet another character that makes up the Narrative-Self.

THE STORY WEAVER

Any observation of the running narrative in your head will almost immediately reveal that it is not simply an around-the-clock problem seeker. It also situates everything about you as well as the world around you within a story. It weaves a chronicle with you in the starring role. At times it will be your strongest advocate, minimize your failures and shortcomings, and maximize your successes and accomplishments. In other moments, it will do the exact opposite and chastise you for your mistakes and shortcomings.

Both of these happen in the background and within the context of an overall story that is constantly mulled over, questioned, probed, and reworked with the hope of it becoming increasingly true. With each revision, the story weaver tries to pass its narrative off as accurate enough to believe in and act upon. We execute on it, even though we know that parts of the stories it tells us are incomplete estimates at best, and outright fiction at worst.

The constant reworking of this overall narrative, along with the virtually endless sub-stories that comprise it, creates a problem over time. Modern neuroscience tells us that memories are not permanently stored in their original form, like the image in a picture. Memories only store things from our perspective. And each time we recall something, it is brought up for revision and then stored again. As our stories are retold, their fictional and accurate elements continue to morph. The original reality of what happened fades even further making our life story increasingly inaccurate over time.

THE CARETAKER

One of the central stories the weaver has spun is that it is your invaluable caretaker. Over time, this part of the narrative becomes so strong that a belief forms at the very heart of 'you' that the Narrative-Self and its essential, guiding, and trusted voice must survive at all costs. It doesn't believe it is trying to make your life a nightmare of ups and downs, rather it sees itself as your best hope for survival and improvement. This isn't surprising given the dominant role it has performed since the earliest days in your life. It truly has been fundamental to shaping your development, both positive and negative.

The story weaver and the problem finder combine with other elements from your Narrative-Self to form a nexus that creates the caretaker. Each contributor is simple and functional on its own, but the interactions among them make *the voice* in your head and what it feels like to be you complicated and produces a great deal of conflict for you, both internally and externally in your life. Together they ensure that no matter what happens, the story weaver will just add it to your overall narrative and work diligently with the problem finder to return you to your standard level of happiness. The weaver will also work hard to make sure that life consists of plenty of ups and downs to keep the problem finder and the rewards of problem solving within reach.

The result of this, and the years of development leading up to this point in your life, is that your Narrative-Self feels like who and what you are. Although no one else hears it, from your perspective it seems to be associated with, and central to, everything you experience. It appears able to separate itself from, analyze, and comment on everything being remembered, imagined, and reported from your senses. This gives the impression that it is different than these other contents of your experience, apart from, and even superior to them. It's no wonder that we mistake this for our true self, who we are. At least until we experience a moment when it falls silent and we realize how much more there is to both us and the world.

CHAPTER 3: THE FINDERS

Perhaps as many as twenty percent of people in Western developed nations have had the Narrative-Self's voice fall completely silent for at least a moment, with maybe half a percent having it become persistently far less influential or leave altogether. This is a massively life-changing event for both groups. Even those who only get a glimpse typically rate it as among the most important and positively transformative events in their lives.

Those who have never experienced it wonder how anyone could continue to function if *the voice* fell completely silent. This doubt is created by Narrative-Self. For example, it is following along as you read this right now and telling you it is impossible to survive without its wise counsel. This shows, once again, how wrong it can be. Our study participants with the highest amount of wellbeing and the greatest sense of freedom typically felt that the absence of *the voice* had vastly improved their performance and ability to function. Far from being a hindrance, the disappearance of Narrative-Self and its voice was the greatest thing that had ever happened to them.

Those who experience a reduction in Narrative-Self often insist that it can't be described with words. This obviously created a major hurdle for the scientific study. To solve it, our research questions forced participants to answer using neutral language that could be readily understood across cultures. This started at the highest-level categories, which delved into cognition (thoughts and thinking), affect (emotion), perception, and memory. These are things that everyone experiences, so changes in them could be easily compared across participants.

When the Narrative-Self lost its importance or fell silent, remarkable things occurred. A deep and Fundamental Wellbeing took root and anxiety, stress, and depression evaporated. The tendency to live in the future or dwell in the past receded, and their awareness became more centered in the present moment. Each moment tended to feel just fine, exactly as it was, no matter what was happening. Despite this, they were still able to skillfully discriminate and navigate the world, perhaps more so than ever before.

Individuals who experience this are no longer caught up in their personal stories, nor do they feel a need to perpetuate them. Their mind is clear, and they aren't subject to the lengthy emotional swings the rest of humanity endures. One of the most surprising things uncovered is that they have a greatly reduced, or even no, fear of death.

Perhaps most importantly, they feel complete. That nagging hole that most people experience at their center vanishes and is replaced by a fundamental contentment as their nearly constant companion. That elusive 'something' others continue to search for—inside themselves with therapy, self-help, or endlessly pursued goals; or outside themselves through relationships or a constant drumbeat of purchased goods and services—these individuals have found. They are no longer on the hunt for what they could add to themselves, because they know, absolutely, that they are whole. Their search is over. This is why the project refers to them *Finders*.

UNDERSTANDING THE FINDERS

Our research sought the answers to several critical questions. Where did these Finders come from? Was there something special about them? What made them this way?

We soon discovered there was no detectable pattern or commonality to how they arrived at Fundamental Wellbeing. A handful believed they had been this way their entire life, but most experienced a shift that brought it about. Sometimes the transition was gradual, other times it happened in an instant. For some, it was an overwhelming moment, others didn't notice it until weeks after it had occurred, or even longer. Some had actively sought out Fundamental Wellbeing, often for years or decades. Others were forced into it from the depths of depression. Still others accidentally stumbled into it and had no idea what had brought it about. Although the way the change occurred differed, they had one thing in common: once it happened, they would not trade what they'd found for anything.

We also learned that it is not a new phenomenon. Because of the promise they hold for the rest of humanity, throughout history volumes have been written about Finders, and by them. Massive institutions that influence much of the world have been built around them. Their ranks comprise some of the most famous people in history. At times they have been venerated, even worshiped. During other periods they've been killed or driven underground.

Through it all, in every epoch of history and culture, they've remained an enigma. Until now, no one has been able to answer even the most basic questions about who they are, how they differ from the rest of us, and if their claims are true. As our research expanded and became more refined, a clearer picture began to emerge with astounding answers to these age-old questions. The most exciting was the discovery that there are steps anyone can take to join them. In fact, all around the world, more and more people are becoming Finders every day.

CHAPTER 4: WHAT FINDERS KNOW THAT YOU DON'T

One of the most surprising changes Finders experience is a fundamental shift in their sense of who they are. Nearly all non-Finders have a story-building, problem-finding Narrative-Self inside that forms the dominant piece of who they assume they are. This was aptly described by one of the research participants as represented by the incessant "blah, blah, blah…" in your head that cares a great deal about your personal story and history.

Behind this voice lies a vast, interconnected series of thoughts and emotions that are being driven by complex interactions between your internal biology and the external world. *The voice* you hear reflects the structure of a deeper, hidden sense of self. When we use positive psychology or self-improvement techniques, we're trying to influence one or more aspects of this hidden structure, hoping that we'll see changes reflected in our interface to it—*the voice*. Unfortunately, most of these methods cannot reach very deep, so they don't have much lasting impact.

The voice is intimately tied to a narrative that it creates to reinforce the feeling that you are a separate and isolated individual. This seems to be the Narrative-Self's most important element. It binds everything together and attempts to present a coherent whole—a unified 'you' that makes sense both internally and to others.

In most people, the Narrative-Self spends a great deal of time seeking the approval of others. This approval is critical to its validity. The Narrative-Self also works hard to increasingly gain a sense of control over the external world that it feels separate and apart from. Both of these functions relate to its problem-solving aspects; however, they also run deeper.

The Narrative-Self is also the part of you that is driven by a fear of death—its death. When its importance lessens, or it is silenced altogether, the fear of death typically reduces or vanishes even though you are still very much alive. This is one of many powerful liberations that occur for Finders.

The Narrative-Self may be so obsessed with seeking approval and fearing death because deep down it knows it is expendable, that it isn't really your deepest or truest self. It constantly seeks to overcome the insecurity this produces by trying to prove that it is something it isn't, that it is who you really are.

The Narrative-Self is also strongly associated with 'its' body as well as 'its' thoughts, emotions, and memories. If you ask the average individual who s/he is, the person will usually begin recounting his or her personal history and the overall story of who s/he is as an individual. Based on our research, the project estimates that over 99.5% of people experience who they are through this narrative form of self.

Finders are not as tightly bound to a narrative-based sense of self. At the very least, the incessant "blah, blah, blah" in their heads has become far less important and is taken nowhere near as seriously. For many Finders, the input *the voice* provides is treated the same way as information from the physical senses: sight, hearing, touch, smell, and taste. When it arises, it is viewed as something that may or may not be relevant, or even accurate. For others, it has largely or totally fallen silent.

Whether reduced or eliminated, this change of relationship to Narrative-Self leaves the mind as a powerful tool that isn't burdened by all that constant chatter. While the rest of the population feels trapped within a deep and persistent sense of insecurity and separation, Finders typically feel more deeply a part of the world around them. They also don't feel as constrained by their physical body. However, these descriptions are far too simple.

CHAPTER 5: THE MANY FLAVORS OF FUNDAMENTAL WELLBEING

Fundamental Wellbeing manifests in many forms. Often, though not always, it is colored by a mix of the culture and belief systems that were absorbed prior to, and in some cases after, it arrived. Consider a religious example involving a Christian, a Buddhist, and an atheist.

For a devout Christian Finder, Fundamental Wellbeing is often experienced as union with the divine, in whatever form. This feels like it extends beyond the physical body. It can be very different from a Buddhist Finder's experience, which might involve a deep and profound sense of spaciousness, although this also feels like it is not limited to the physical body. However, within the divine the Christian will often also feel a profound sense of depth and spaciousness that is not entirely different from the Buddhist.

The same can be true for atheist Finders. They are likely to feel Fundamental Wellbeing as a deep connection to their environment, or nature. This is experienced as having a sense of self that seems like it somehow extends beyond the physical body and to the world that surrounds it. As with the Christian and Buddhist Finders, this expansion most likely also involves a newfound sense of spaciousness, and a change in relationship with space itself.

Each of these individuals has similar elements that show up and are interpreted, emphasized, or de-emphasized differently depending upon their worldview and what it values. While their religious beliefs are highlighted in this example, a wide range of other factors also shape the experience. Biology, cultural influences, and a Finder's day-to-day lifestyle all play a part, as do many other things.

THE FINDER AND THE NARRATIVE-SELF

Over time, as dirt accumulates on a window, the view changes. A once bright and beautiful scene can become increasingly dull and less appealing to the eye. The window and view remain the same; the only difference is the layer of dirt that is accumulating. Once the window is cleaned, the beautiful scene beyond it returns.

The Narrative-Self can be thought of as being like dirt that accumulates on the glass of your worldview. It is a dynamic and ever-changing filter that all perceptions, thoughts, memories, and so on pass through. Its problem-finding, insecure, and fearful nature colors and distorts our moment-to-moment experience. As it is reduced in importance, or when it seems to leave entirely, a fundamental contentment, peace, and wellbeing increasingly bubble up. Although this may be the first time a person remembers experiencing these things at this degree of intensity, they aren't being created—just uncovered like the beauty that was already waiting beyond the dirt.

The change is typically so profound that Finders stop obsessively identifying with their life history. It's common to hear them refer to it as a "story," one in which they have a reduced, and even little-to-no personal investment or attachment. For some, it's almost as if they are more of a spectator than a participant, though a richer and even fuller life continues for them beyond the shift.

A FINDER BY ANY OTHER NAME

Given the central role that religion and spirituality have played throughout human history, it's not surprising that many forms of Fundamental Wellbeing have been discovered and cultivated by them over time. For some of these, the shift is of such importance that they ritualize the transition into this new way of being by requiring new Finders to change their name. Often there are specific rules for how this name is selected. For example, it may be provided by a key leader or spiritual advisor.

A small minority of Finders change their name even when they are not in a tradition that recommends it. There are several reasons for this.

A great deal of internal psychological conditioning is associated with their former name. Continuing to use it can cause this to be triggered, and slightly impact their level of wellbeing. While over time this will extinguish, some don't want to wait for that to happen.

Alternatively, for some the transition to Fundamental Wellbeing is more profound than others. These Finders can feel that their birth name reflects an identity that is no longer relevant, or even present. They may choose spiritual or religious names, in an effort to describe or convey their new way of experiencing the world. Or, they might simply begin to use their middle name, or select another secular name.

For quite some time, it appeared that this change in the sense of self might be the only common element within Fundamental Wellbeing. As our research progressed, other similarities began to emerge and form a rich tapestry that more fully described the experience. To understand how it all weaves together, we have to step back a bit in time and consider how the research project evolved.

CHAPTER 6: HOW IT ALL STARTED

This research began in 2006 as an inquiry into what types of people might have the most wellbeing, and how others could rise to their level. Over time, Finders came to the foreground as the preeminent group to study. At the time, few within the academic world were interested in Fundamental Wellbeing, and many were openly hostile towards researching it. It was viewed as a fringe area where ridiculous and impossible assertions were being made by potential research participants, including claims that didn't seem testable by science.

We started by exploring what had already been done by contacting the small number of academic researchers who were already interested in Fundamental Wellbeing. Usually these individuals were in university religion or philosophy departments, but there were a handful of psychology and neuroscience researchers. I traveled to meet as many of them as possible to discuss their work, and read everything that was available from these corners of the academy. To avoid strategic mistakes that would prevent the research results from being taken seriously, sympathetic senior academics were consulted about the best path forward. They advised beginning with *gold-standard* psychological measures to try to determine what might make Finders different from the rest of the population.

You may have taken some of these tests at school or work, or possibly even online for fun. They are paper and pencil or computer administered sets of questions, usually with multiple-choice answers. The phrase gold-standard means measures that have been extensively used and are considered reliable by the portion of the academic world that specializes in them. Each of the initial participants was sent the first batch of gold standard measures, followed by as many additional batches as s/he would fill out. The measures included ones for: personality, anxiety, depression, psychopathology, wellbeing, various types of development, mystical experience, and more.

This was a very exciting time because of the groundbreaking nature of the research being undertaken. Here was a group of people who made so many astonishing claims about their experience of the world. Now, it seemed like the project was on the precipice of peeling back the first layer of mystery surrounding who they were and what made them special. When the results finally came in, this emotional high made the results all the more disappointing.

As the measures were scored, an immediate and straightforward pattern emerged. The initial respondents had high wellbeing, low neuroticism, and claimed little to no depression, stress, and anxiety. There were no other shared combinations of personality traits or psychological factors that separated them from the general population.

In short, the results showed that the participants were, essentially, normal and happy. Nothing was found to uniquely identify them as a group, or help objectively confirm or disprove their claims of Fundamental Wellbeing. For a scientist seeking measurable results, this was very disappointing. Either the critics within the academy were correct, and these individuals were lying or delusional, or we were missing something.

CHAPTER 7: FINDING THE FINDERS

At the time, we didn't realize that the project had stumbled on one of the most interesting and baffling facts about Finders. Despite the significant change that has occurred in how they experience life, others often don't notice. It's not just the traditional academic measures that miss the change that has occurred. More often than not, so do the people around the Finder.

Externally, Finders retain who they are to such an extent that even the people closest to them, including family and close friends, often don't detect that a shift has occurred. Unsure of what to make of their newfound experience of themselves and the world, Finders frequently don't tell anyone about their massive internal change. Depending on how it unfolds, those close to the new Finder may notice that the person has been in a great mood lately, is less reactive, and is even unusually kind and thoughtful. These are typically just interpreted as a good period in the relationship, not as an indicator of deeper change. The only universal exception are Finders who were depressed prior to their transition. In these cases, the personality differences are so profound that those close to them generally take notice.

How could people who claim to have experienced such a profound internal shift still seem the same to those around them? As our research progressed, the project discovered that Finders' knowledge and history are intact and fully usable. In fact, without the story weaver's spin clouding their minds, everything often becomes more usable. The personality and its direction, set by years of conditioning, seems to simply keep moving forward. Except in unusual cases, the things that make another person 'who they are' from the outside remain largely intact.

Although this will usually change over time as their previous psychological conditioning begins to extinguish, for the first year or two they typically still dress the same, talk the same, and even have the same sense of morality. They generally retain the same habits (including

31

'bad' ones, like smoking), food preferences, political views, hobbies, skills, and so forth. If they were concerned about the environment the day before, they continue to hand out flyers at Earth Day events after their transition. If not, they still drive their gas-guzzling SUV or cruise around in their private jet and think nothing of it.

This extends to the workplace. The shift to Fundamental Wellbeing rarely seems to occur while someone is at their place of employment. Since they feel so different, many new Finders are uncertain about how their next work shift will go. Much to their surprise, their co-workers typically do not notice any difference, and it is just another day at the office. This has been reported by Finders across a wide range of positions, from creative work to engineering, and from high-level leadership roles to hourly manual labor and service jobs.

If losing your Narrative-Self worries you because you don't know who you'll be, or what your life will be like after the shift, the answer seems to be: pretty much the same as you are now, except with an unimaginable level of contentment and wellbeing (even if you already think of yourself as very happy).

A minority of people profoundly change as part of the transition. Some aspects of the conditioning that comprise who they are shift radically, and immediately. They may have dramatic adjustments to their morality, especially if they were engaged in behavior their culture defined as 'bad' prior to it. Habits viewed as negative, such as drinking, drug use, or smoking might immediately fall away and not return. Forced changes to diets can also occur. Less healthy meals can suddenly become difficult to keep down, forcing a change to more nutritious food. One Finder, who previously would have gotten winded climbing a flight of stairs at sea level, over a period of three years lost sixty pounds and took up high-elevation mountain hiking. Finders might also undergo an intense religious or spiritual experience that results in conversion to a new faith tradition, or a recommitment to or departure from an existing one.

During this phase of the research, we realized that what was happening in Finders was not being detected by the standard measures used in psychology, and why. Virtually all gold-standard measures target the Narrative-Self. This isn't surprising, because psychology has considered this the 'real self' for over a century, so of course that's what it studies.

This was exciting, because it meant that the project might be exploring new territory. Of course, the other option was still possible. It could be that Fundamental Wellbeing wasn't real, or that we had not found people to research who actually experienced it. A new approach was needed. It was time to sit down and speak with some of the research participants face-to-face.

CHAPTER 8: WHAT 12 HOURS IN SOMEONE'S LIVING ROOM CAN TEACH YOU ABOUT THEM

Ironically, the first interview didn't take place with one of the individuals who had completed the measures. While visiting my hometown, I stumbled across an old acquaintance of twenty years. It turned out that in the intervening years, this highly respected physician had not only lost his family and wealth, but had even been to jail because of a problem with addiction. In prison, he had his first taste of Fundamental Wellbeing. Realizing what it offered, he worked hard to both refine and stabilize it during his short stay in "camp," followed by a six-month meditation retreat and a few more months camping in the wilderness.

His high intelligence and extensive knowledge of psychology and physiology allowed him to speak lucidly about his ongoing experience of Fundamental Wellbeing. He freely, openly, and thoughtfully answered every question put to him. It was the project's first deep and extended glimpse into the internal world of a Finder, and it was remarkable.

As the initial pool of interviewees expanded, it became clear that not everyone would be as open about their Fundamental Wellbeing as my friend. The next set of interviews was with spiritual teachers and venerated members of religious communities.

For thousands of years, religious traditions have served as a key cultural institution. When kingdoms and empires fell, they remained. Even in the modern era, our universities were religious institutions before the German research model was introduced in the 1800's. They have been instrumental in preserving knowledge of our past and guiding humanity's future.

As part of this, most religious traditions have systematically uncovered, explored, and preserved knowledge about various types of Fundamental Wellbeing. In Christianity, individuals who experience it are generally referred to as mystics. At times they have been exalted, at others burned at the stake. Islam and Judaism have had a similarly rocky relationship with Finders. Buddhism and Hinduism have been more kind, typically viewing Fundamental Wellbeing as the pinnacle of human existence. Knowledge of it has also been cultivated, revered, and preserved in numerous native and indigenous religious, spiritual, and psychological systems.

From the perspective of these venerated religious leaders, I was just another in a long line of people inquiring about their inner experience. They were kind enough to answer my questions, but didn't really explore them with me like my old friend did. Most didn't seem to regard the scientific investigation of Fundamental Wellbeing as likely to be any more fruitful or valid than did the critics within the academy.

Nonetheless, the information they provided was valuable. The first details began to emerge that showed Finders experienced the world in similar ways to each other, yet very differently from the rest of the population. As strangers from different cultures answered the same question in the same way, validation of what each was sharing began to build.

This period provided something absolutely critical. Now there was a growing set of answers to compare with others' responses. It allowed the research to be extended to people who made claims involving Fundamental Wellbeing that didn't have a large community to back them up and provide additional credibility. Initially, these Finders were often less well-known spiritual teachers. Like my doctor friend, they were usually open and forthright.

In time, the participant pool expanded to include people living routine lives. Usually these individuals weren't public about their Fundamental Wellbeing. These participants represented an important breakthrough in the research. We began learning how Fundamental Wellbeing manifested in an ordinary person's life. This allowed us to begin asking some very important questions. What, if anything, changed for them over time? How did it affect their job, their family and friends, and other aspects of their life?

The focus shifted to finding as many of these Finders as possible. In 2009, a close friend and I co-authored a quasi-fictional book, *The Fourth*

Awakening—now a bestselling series—that was designed to attract them. The hope was that this book would reach an even wider cross-section of Finders, and that they would get in touch with us. I also spoke widely and did media interviews about the project to publicize it.

Slowly, through word of mouth, it became easier to locate participants. During this period another important discovery was made. When you come across one Finder in the general populace, it is almost certain that they will be in communication with one or two others. The experience of Fundamental Wellbeing can be very isolating. A Finder's best bet for support often comes from materials other Finders have produced, and from interacting with other Finders. Most have found at least one other Finder to talk with about it.

THE INTERVIEW FORMAT

Early on, a standard formula for interviews was developed. Each would begin by asking about personal history and how the Finder came to Fundamental Wellbeing. This would present the opportunity to get to know the person, build rapport, and uncover the language s/he preferred to use when describing it. Next came the main data gathering phase of the interview. The Finder would be asked a series of questions, beginning with ones involving changes in cognition (thoughts and thinking), followed by others involving emotion, perception, and memory.

One of the great strengths of this interview process was that there were no 'correct' answers available. Since no one had previously asked these types of questions to Finders, and they were not revealed or discussed publicly during the interview phase of the research project, their reliability was greatly enhanced. The data being collected was new, and originating from within each individual in response to the questions being asked. While a participant might know some others in the study, s/he could not know many, especially given the global diversity of the population being researched.

The interviews were long. Six to twelve hours was not uncommon. Considering how difficult it was to locate a Finder who was willing to talk, the interviews often lasted until a person kicked us out of their living room, or all the local restaurants and coffee shops we could meet in had closed. To maximize the accuracy of the data, as well as the rapport built with participants, all interviews were conducted in person. The vast majority were done in someone's home, though they would last so long that walks, going out to eat, and similar venue changes were common. Most participants were only interviewed once. As the interviews continued, an entire landscape emerged that was nothing short of amazing, and something that we never imagined when the project started.

PART 2 – THE CONTINUUM

"There are no differences but differences of degree between different degrees of difference and no difference."
William James

CHAPTER 9: THE CONTINUUM EMERGES

While each research participant had a unique and personal story, it was clear early on that there were many underlying similarities in the experiences being reported. One of our biggest concerns was falling into a trap of prematurely thinking these similarities were more than just coincidental. For an extended period of time we simply listened, categorized, and reflected upon the information being collected. The focus was on ways to refine the data collection process and trying to discover better ways to probe ever more deeply for relevant information.

After just a few dozen interviews, it became impossible to ignore these patterns. Multiple clusters of related experiences were clearly revealing themselves. In a conscious effort to avoid loaded terms like stages or levels, initially these collections of similar data were placed in what the project called *buckets*. Each data bucket grouped Finders together based on the way they reported experiencing both their sense of self and the world. Another revelation was that many participants reported their Fundamental Wellbeing had changed over time. When these changes were examined, it became clear that some Finders had more deeply settled in to their existing bucket, while others moved to a different bucket entirely.

As the interviews continued and the raw data was better understood, a pattern began to emerge. Over time it became apparent that these clusters were ways of experiencing life that fell along a single path, a specifically ordered *continuum* of related conscious experiences. At that point, the buckets were renamed to *locations*, with the idea being that they were spots along a single continuum of possible experiences.

| Location 1 | Location 2 | Location 3 | Location 4 | Location 5+ |

To make this concept easy to visualize, the locations were given a position on a straight-line graph. Imagine the locations stretched out in a straight line, with each getting a number to identify it. In this book, the continuum will be divided up into Locations 1, 2, 3, 4, and 5+. The continuum starts at Location 1, and progresses from there. Finders who were at Location 2 were most likely to transition to Location 3 or Location 1, rather than skipping over to, say, Location 4.

Not many Finders seem to have reached beyond Location 4. Fewer still have made it to even further later locations, such as Location 9. As a result, it is difficult to uncover patterns and similarities in these later locations on the continuum. At this stage of our research, we're not even sure how many locations there might be. Currently we think more than twenty, and that many locations have yet to be precisely mapped. Since the vast majority of Finders are in Locations 1 through 4, that is the focus of this book. Once the locations had revealed their order, an overall theme emerged. Each higher numbered location seemed to bring a greater reduction in the Narrative-Self, and higher wellbeing.

While the image of a string of locations along a line is great for initially grasping the concept of the continuum, it also hides a great deal of complexity. Everyone in a location does not experience Fundamental Wellbeing the exact same way. Rather, locations collect together related experiences of Fundamental Wellbeing. In this sense they are best thought of as being similar to geographical regions.

Imagine a region of the world viewed on a map. It may have a variety of terrain, distinctive cities that range from large to small, and rural populations in outlying areas. If you were to jump to the other side of Earth, it would be similar but not the same. It would have a variety of unique cities, very or only slightly different terrain, different language and cultures, and so forth. Often, regions that are next to each other are more alike where they meet, while the further one goes from that common boundary the more differences begin to appear. This is a good way to begin to think about the locations on the continuum.

It's important to visualize the continuum as one continuous expression. Most, though not all, of the variations between locations are not dramatic night-and-day-type differences. Often one location fades and blends into the next.

Just as you can be on the far end of the continuum, you can also be on the far end of a location. The experience of Fundamental Wellbeing there can be much closer to the location it borders, rather than an earlier portion of the location it is a part of. For example, someone might find him or herself within the 'region' of Location 2. If s/he landed closer to Location 1, the person's experience would tend to be more similar to it than, say, Location 3. Conversely, if someone landed at the far end of Location 2, his or her experience would be more likely to be shaded towards Location 3 than Location 1.

It's more complicated than this because culture, genetics, and much more can affect someone's experience of a location. To return to our map analogy, imagine two very different regions. One is by the ocean, another in the mountains. Despite these differences, both have a major city, suburbs of that city, and smaller towns. Inhabitants of a region can live in any of these options. They can also move between them, either on short trips or for longer periods. They might even choose to live for a few years in one village, and then move to the city. Regardless of where they live, people in a given region still describe themselves with the fundamental commonalities that come with living in that region. Yet, even with these similarities, the cultural differences between living in the city or the country can be stark. Locations are like this as well. Although everyone in a specific location shares a more-or-less common way of describing Fundamental Wellbeing, there are shades of differences between them. However, their descriptions differ considerably when compared with Finders in other locations.

TRANSITIONING TO AND MOVING ALONG THE CONTINUUM

When a person transitions into Fundamental Wellbeing, s/he seems to be able to initially "land" in any location from 1 to 4. None of the research participants' starting position on the continuum was Location 5 or later, though it certainly might be possible and just not something that has been uncovered yet. Movement between locations can be either 'forward' (toward Location 5+) or 'backward' (toward Location 1).

Keep in mind that terms like 'forward' and 'backward' are arbitrary labels and are not meant to connote any sense of higher or lower value. All locations can be viewed as having equal value. Each brings its own way of experiencing Fundamental Wellbeing. As we will see later, individuals who have experienced multiple locations on the continuum often have examples from their life that do not necessarily match up with the idea of 'forward,' 'higher,' or 'further' being 'better' or 'worse.'

It's not unusual for Finders to feel that they have completely left the Narrative-Self behind during their transition to Fundamental Wellbeing. They are often surprised when transitions to later locations on the continuum reveal parts of the Narrative-Self that were hidden but had continued to be there all along. Often, these only become apparent as they are falling away during the shift to the new location. After a few of these transitions, most Finders reach the conclusion that there are probably many more aspects of the Narrative-Self that remain hidden from view, and that they can expect to have these be revealed and fall away as their deepening on the continuum continues.

DEEPENING INTO A LOCATION

Almost all Finders agreed that their initial transition was just the beginning of a process that seemed to be able to unfold, and deepen, endlessly—a never-ending adventure. The phrase, 'deepening in a location' can be used in one of two ways. Sometimes it means the length of time spent in a certain spot within a location (a sub-location, like a specific village in a region). For example, someone might initially transition into the early end of a location and, over time, become more solidly established in that location.

Deepening can also refer to progressing further on the continuum, towards the later end of the Finder's current location, though this is probably best referred to as either 'progressing' or 'moving on or along' the continuum. This movement follows a very logical and easy to understand pattern. For example, Finders in Location 1 still have a relatively full range of positive and negative emotions. While those at the early end of Location 2 also still experience a mix of emotions, they are biased much more towards the positive. As Finders move further along in Location 2 the positive nature of their emotions continues to increase. By the 'far end' of Location 2 they almost exclusively experience positive emotions. They are also probably getting glimpses of what Location 3 is like.

DEGREES OF DIFFERENCE

The research data can easily be grouped into many different degrees of locations. Sub-locations, for example, could be treated as locations themselves. In that case, there would be many more locations on the continuum in what is being called Locations 1 through 4. In most cases, though, these sub-locations merely represent a slight difference of degree within a given location.

Many religious and spiritual systems that have charted parts of this terrain use maps that embody a finer grain of detail like this. However, it all seems to sort itself most clearly at the highest level into the broader categories used in this book. Grouped this way, we've found it to be a more universally useful and helpful model for Finders to work with in understanding where they've been, where they are, and where they might find themselves at another point in their lives. It becomes a bit too complicated and confusing for people when it is divided into smaller chunks, unless someone is primarily interested in just that part of the terrain.

Unlike these higher-level categories, finer grain ones don't seem to be as linear. In other words, Finders don't have to pass through all or even most sub-locations in a given higher-level location, such as Location 2, in order to transition to the next higher-level location. A Finder can force themselves to do this, but the data suggests that this slows down their progression to the next location.

Many religions and spiritual systems focus on only a limited subset of locations. These types of systems often seek to very precisely tune the experience of both progression, and what they consider the ultimate final spot to arrive at on the continuum. These types of systems believe it makes sense to be more granular on the portions of the continuum they focus on, and they often view other locations as invalid.

REACTIONS TO THE CONTINUUM

When they learn about the continuum, Finders typically have one of three reactions. Many contact the project and thank us for providing materials that finally contextualize their life experience. Quite a few Finders transition in relative isolation and have no experience of Fundamental Wellbeing other than their own. They are often deeply grateful to know that others have experienced things similar to what they have. Another commonality is for people to have been involved in one or more religious or spiritual system, witness others transition to types of Fundamental Wellbeing that are not part of that tradition, and become confused. These Finders are typically very appreciative for the context that the continuum provides. Overall, when it comes to Fundamental Wellbeing, it seems to be helpful to have the perspective the continuum offers.

Others write to tell us that we got one or more location correct, but clearly don't understand Fundamental Wellbeing if we feel that the other locations are also a part of it. For example, people with a strong belief in Location 2's form of nonduality often criticize us for including Location 1 in the continuum. Individuals who transitioned directly into Location 4 and deepened there are often the harshest critics, and generally feel that Location 4 is the only valid form of Fundamental Wellbeing, at least until they shift either forward or back on the continuum.

Still other Finders have little to no interest in the continuum at all. This is not surprising. In our academic work, the project uses terms like Ongoing or Persistent forms of Non-Symbolic Experience (ONE or PNSE) to describe Fundamental Wellbeing. These terms didn't emerge from the data, rather they were adapted for practical reasons from a phrase used by a developmental psychology researcher at Harvard, Susanne Cook-Greuter. Simply put, they resonated with prospective participants and made them more likely to join the research.

The term *Non-Symbolic* sums up the way many Finders feel about a shift that has happened within their cognition. Some portions of the mind involving the Narrative-Self like to turn everything into a symbol so it can be manipulated, communicated, and so forth. As we'll see, Finders feel that they experience a more direct perception of reality that includes a reduction in these symbolic layers of perception and analysis. This makes some of them hesitant to want to explore their Fundamental Wellbeing from within a symbolic system—like the conceptual framework of the continuum.

Though it's taken many years to reach this point, future work will undoubtedly produce changes to this model and continue to refine it. For example, it's possible that this single continuum will be broken up into sub-components that reflect the primary underlying categories of cognition, emotion, perception, and memory. Or, perhaps a vertical dimension will be added that will reflect another aspect of subjective experience, such as depth within a specific point on the continuum.

For now, the important thing is that this current form of the continuum has been refined and found useful by Finders worldwide. The next five chapters summarize the key traits of each location for easy reference. The information they contain is highly condensed, so don't worry if you can't understand it all in detail yet. The rest of the book adds a great deal of additional information and context.

If you find the chapters in the rest of this section are too abbreviated, feel free to just skip them for now and read them before you begin Part 4. Part 3 dives in-depth into each of the core aspects of Fundamental Wellbeing as they relate to each location, including the changes in: sense of self, cognition, emotion, perception, and memory. If you read the rest of Part 2 now, coming back and re-reading it after you finish with Part 3 can also help you put all the details provided up to that point into place.

CHAPTER 10: LOCATION 1

Location 1 individuals are on the earliest portion of the continuum. As with every location, the Finders here can come from any walk of life. They may be highly educated or illiterate, of high social status or homeless, young or old. They might have experienced a dramatic, instantaneous shift into Fundamental Wellbeing, or have transitioned more gradually. The shift into Location 1 can be so subtle that, remarkably, sometimes it isn't detected until a while after it has occurred. This is especially the case if the person was already happy.

The most telltale sign of Fundamental Wellbeing at Location 1 is a newfound sense that everything is fundamentally fine. This sense of "fundamental okayness" is usually in the background of experience at Location 1, which is how it can go unnoticed in people who already had high wellbeing. The transition doesn't prevent negative emotions from arising, but it does change an individual's relationship with these emotions.

A serious life event, such as the death of a parent, departure of a spouse, or loss of a career can still produce significant negative emotion. However, despite present circumstances, a Location 1 Finder is able to look within to a deeper level that somehow seems okay. Because this level seems to always be there, it can appear to be the most "true" part of their reality. This can make the external world and their former experience of a Narrative-Self seem less real, and sometimes even "not real," by comparison.

Although this sense of fundamental okayness usually remains in the background for Location 1 Finders, there are moments when it moves into the foreground and seems to infuse all experience of the world. The possibility of it remaining there becomes very enticing, and Finders often begin to experiment to see if they can bring it forward more often. This can produce movement along the continuum to later portions of Location 1, and eventually a transition into Location 2.

The transition to Fundamental Wellbeing also brings a reduction in the influence of the Narrative-Self, or the feeling that it has been lost altogether. After the transition, Finders' minds seem quieter because of a reduction in the quantity, emotional strength, and / or "stickiness" of Narrative-Self related thoughts. This can make their mind, and the world around them, seem like it has an underlying "silence" and "stillness" that was not previously noticed. It can also produce a profound sense of foundational and interpenetrating "spaciousness."

Location 1 Finders experience a heightened sense of being complete. If they were previously on a quest for meaning, deep truths, answers to life's big questions, or ways to fill the "God-sized hole" within them, this search has mostly, or even entirely, come to an end. If their hold on Location 1 is a bit tenuous, this sense may not have fully matured in them yet, and they can still feel some aspects of seeking. Generally, this manifests as a desire to deepen into Location 1 or progress further on the continuum, and thus stabilize their sense of Fundamental Wellbeing. These Finders might feel like they are "oscillating" in and out of Fundamental Wellbeing as conditioning arises within them, but this is usually not actually the case.

Alternatively, if their transition to Location 1 was more intense, they probably have a profound sense that they have found, and are experiencing, the "Truth." These Finders discover their worries and fears seem to have manifested from their now weakened, or seemingly absent, Narrative-Self. Fear is largely gone, and this can even include the fear of death.

Location 1 individuals notice that their focus is now more centered in the present moment, rather than the past or future. Memories spontaneously arise less often, causing these Finders to sometimes believe that they are experiencing problems with their memory, though that is usually not the case. They are still able to encode (store) and recall information at a level that would be expected for their age and health status. Memories are simply arising less on their own. Because these Finders have become less attached to the story of their life, they are also less likely to actively call up as many memories as they did before their transition.

It's not just their personal story that has become less interesting. One of the things most Finders notice first is a reduction in their interest in nearly all stories. This can manifest in a number of ways. News junkies may find themselves much less interested in the news. TV series and movie lovers find themselves increasingly less drawn to these forms of passing the time.

Perhaps most importantly, Location 1 Finders often become much less interested in the stories the people around them tell. It becomes clear that culture and human interaction is deeply story based. They may notice less interest in their friends, co-workers, and even their family members, and try to get them to interact in ways that are more interesting to Finders. This doesn't go unnoticed, and is often not a welcomed change.

Sometimes this can lead to increased isolation that is self-imposed but viewed as more desirable than having a lot of story driven, approval-seeking conversations. Relationships generally do adapt, but it is also common for old friends to drift away and new ones to enter the picture that are more aligned with the Finder's new relationship preferences.

The peace and contentment that accompanies Fundamental Wellbeing can be suppressed by psychological triggers, but usually it recovers rapidly once the stimulus is removed. Over time, repeated exposure to the same stimulus can cause less of this suppression to occur. Location 1 Finders still experience a range of positive and negative emotions. However, the negative emotions are much more transient and do not have the power over them that they once did. Past psychological conditioning can still trigger thought streams and strong emotional responses, but these usually pass in a matter of moments. Stronger emotional triggers, such as those involving close family, can persist longer.

At Location 1, a Finder's sense of self often becomes larger and feels like it expands beyond the physical body. This varies from one individual to the next and can be anywhere from very subtle, to highly noticeable. There can also be a new sense of connectedness between what was formerly perceived as distinctly separate internal and external worlds. For new Finders, especially those with strong religious underpinnings, there may also be an increased sense of connectedness to the divine and a newly invigorated sense of truth around their religious doctrine. A level of wellbeing is experienced that previously could not have been imagined, regardless of how happy they were previously. They often have a noetic sense that everything is unfolding exactly as it should.

Unless they were significantly depressed just prior to their transition, their outward personality often changes very little. Speech patterns, morals, habits, hobbies, and even addictions probably remain. Physiological ailments most likely remain as well. Those around them probably do not spot the significant amount of change that has occurred.

The experience of physical pain changes, and may be significantly reduced. The Narrative-Self's worry and fear are exerting less of an influence in interpreting the pains and giving it added strength. Drugs for ailments that were previously assumed to be psychological may still be required. This is particularly true for conditions such as anxiety and associated tremors. For example, medication may still be needed to help the body stop shaking, even though the level of anxiety is reported as greatly diminished or completely gone.

In some cases, there may be a detectable change in the person's sense of humor, especially involving analogies and putting others down. New Finders are probably still in the habit of laughing at a broad range of things, especially in social situations, even if internally the motivation isn't as strong as it was previously. They can choose to retain this conditioning for social reasons, though often it feels linked to aspects of the Narrative-Self and thus not desirable. At the same time, a new form of humor begins to emerge, one which sees much of what is directly experienced in life as quite peculiar and funny when paid close attention to.

Goals can abruptly change or remain the same out of habit or after careful re-analysis, depending on how the transition to Fundamental Wellbeing affected their underlying motivations. Whether old or new, the attachment to them and specific outcomes in general is reduced. There can be a deep sense that everything is perfect as it is. This can lead to reduced motivation to do things in day-to-day life until a new sense of motivation takes hold. The latter can take from a few months to just over two years.

It is common for Finders who initially cross over into Location 1 to have a strong, even burning, desire to help others experience Fundamental Wellbeing, versus those who land in Locations 2 or 4. They may make a significant life change that reorients them in this direction, especially if they were deeply unhappy or depressed prior to their transition. They might also change other aspects of their life, usually around triggers that push down their inner feeling of peace and wellbeing. These can be quite dramatic and include: divorce, job or career changes, moving to a new location, and so forth.

Paradoxes can occur around the sense of completeness and other core aspects of Fundamental Wellbeing. These are dealt with in various ways. They can be denied, tolerated, ignored, or reasoned out. Although these types of paradoxes can cause intense psychological suffering for others, this is typically not the case for Finders.

Location 1 Finders often still have conditioning that relates to approval from others. This form of social give and take can trigger them, and will sometimes be experienced as deep hurt. In those who have this residual conditioning, social interaction often remains more fluid and natural when compared with other Finders.

CHAPTER 11: LOCATION 2

While each of the locations has it's own distinctive elements, there are often commonalities across them. What was covered in Location 1—around goals, a present moment focus, feeling complete or whole, relationship to stories, psychological triggers, a sense of self that extends beyond the body, personality changes (or lack thereof), perception of physical pain, humor, goals, and paradoxes—should largely be seen as holding true for later locations unless it is specifically commented upon. Accordingly, many of the things Location 1 Finders experience remain the same or deepen in Location 2.

In Location 2 Finders experience a further reduction in their Narrative-Self related thoughts, and in the emotional content of most of the ones that remain. In other words, these types of thoughts that endure have even less capability to draw them in. This further deepens and increases their immersion in the present moment. It also makes them even less reactive.

The deep sense that everything is fundamentally okay regardless of current circumstances moves more into the foreground the deeper someone moves into Location 2. Towards the furthest reaches of this location, it infuses experience most of the time. This is viewed as one of the best elements of the Location 2 experience.

Location 2 individuals also have fewer and less powerful conditioned psychological responses. Conditioning around needing the approval of others is dissolving, and may result in less social, and socially desirable, behavior. The range of emotions these individuals experience becomes increasingly positive, and negative emotions become less frequent.

In Location 2, the boundaries between what feels like you and what feels like outside of you increasingly soften or disappear entirely. One popular term for this change in perception is nonduality, or "not two." When this is experienced, there is a sense that everything is truly just one thing. This significant change in what it feels like to be 'you' can arrive with a shift in agency. It may feel as if actions are part of a larger universal order, rather than personal. It might even feel as if something larger than 'you' is making decisions and taking action through you.

Location 2 Finders are more likely to intuitively feel that there is a correct decision or path to take when presented with choices, even if there seems to be very little rationality behind the direction being taken. Our experiments suggest that this intuition can be externally influenced. In other words, although this seems to be a further and deeper manifestation of the noetic sense that appears at Location 1, it does not appear to actually be a pathway to a special kind of truth. Despite this, even when this is demonstrated to Location 2 Finders, the internal pull is sufficiently strong that it is often difficult to resist.

Individuals who transition to this location from Location 1 are likely to experience an increase in their sense of peace and wellbeing. Deepening towards Location 3 will result in eventually reaching a point where negative emotions are only rarely experienced. As a Finder gets closer to Location 3, their internal emotional makeup is almost exclusively positive.

CHAPTER 12: LOCATION 3

Location 3 Finders have been freed from a considerable amount of their psychological conditioning and negative emotions. The experience of present moment awareness, inner peace, and wellbeing continues to grow and deepen. In most of Location 3, only one dominant emotion is experienced. It feels like a mixture of various highly positive emotions and feelings such as compassion, joy, and love. These feel like facets of a single meta-emotion.

Though some facets are more active at times than others, this single meta-emotion itself is a near constant experience and companion at Location 3. The emotion is not personal. Facets such as love are felt as divine or universal, or at a minimum, impersonal. Parts of negative emotions are still occasionally felt but only rarely fully form, and generally only in earlier portions of the location as a result of the triggering of very deep and powerful psychological conditioning.

Individuals in Location 3 have less Narrative-Self related thought than those at Locations 1 or 2, though they might notice what remains of it more. The reason for this was aptly summed up by one Finder who noted that in an almost total absence of "suffering," the bit that remains "looms large." When living moment-to-moment in a place of Fundamental Wellbeing, anything that disturbs it, however minor, is difficult to miss. These few remaining thoughts and triggers are one such disturbance.

Location 3 seems to be experienced in two different ways. For many Finders, there is a strong sense of divinity associated with the experience. Other Finders do not report feeling any divinity at all. For them, there is a sense of an all-pervasive consciousness, what philosophers call a *panpsychist* experience. The sense of nonduality or 'oneness' that is felt in Location 2 shifts. As one deepens into Location 3, a sense of deep connectedness and union enter the picture. Union is not possible if you are just one thing, so a subtle sense of self and other returns at this location.

For example, Christian Finders often feel strongly united or merged with Jesus, the Holy Spirit, God, or the Trinity depending upon their sect. A panpsychist-oriented Finder may feel this same deep union involving an all-pervasive consciousness. This location and the sense of union that accompanies it feels amazing, and it is viewed as the pinnacle of spiritual or religious experience in many traditions.

Location 3 Finders are typically delightful to be around. Although their need for approval has lessened even further than Location 2, they often value helping others and work to maintain social graces that allow them to do that. If you had to choose to live in a community of individuals from only one location on the continuum, you'd most likely want it to be people in Location 3.

There are exceptions, however. For a minority of Location 3 Finders, their profound sense of "Truth" involving what should be done in most situations can be so strong that it can make them difficult to live with. Roommates and spouses can find what seem like irrational and imposing demands to be a common annoyance, and their counter perspectives met with unyielding expectations by the Finder.

This mostly happens with Location 3 individuals who have lived in relative isolation from other Finders. In many cases, Finders in this situation have deepened on the continuum while needing to hide their inner experience of Fundamental Wellbeing from those around them. Internally, Finders in this situation will often defer to their inner compass as what is true, and discount the views and opinions of other people in their life who don't seem to share or understand their way of experiencing the world. When combined with the deep sense of "Truth" that typically accompanies Location 3, over time this can lead to a form of intolerance. Because of the general nature of Location 3 it is often only experienced by those closest to the Finder. Others typically still find them a delight to be around.

Location 3 Finders sense that things are fundamentally okay is not only almost always in the foreground, but has been turbocharged. They can feel like a "blessing" is radiating out to everyone in their presence. The world is seen as having a profound degree of perfection. There is a sense that it cannot be any other way than it is at this moment, and that it is exactly as it was meant to be.

Paradoxically, this does not make Location 3 Finders less likely to be activists or people out to change the world. They may still be working on environmental causes, and can be very passionate about helping others reach Fundamental Wellbeing. In some cases these behaviors are just old conditioning and programming that slowly wear off over time. In others, this seems to be more deeply engrained, though they remain less attached to outcome. Although they may still be handing out flyers on Earth Day, when queried privately about it they say, "Well, you know, everything is really perfectly fine, but it wouldn't hurt if we took better care of the environment."

Finders who progress to this point from Location 1 or 2 report increased levels of peace and wellbeing. Individuals at this location often feel that it must be the peak of wellbeing that is possible for a human to experience. Many of the positive traits and types of human experience the project tracked psychologically were most associated with this location.

Fundamental Wellbeing. This is especially true if a Finder transitions to Location 4 from a previous location. These individuals take one of two paths. Some turn back towards earlier locations on the continuum. These *Fluid 4's* often gain the capacity to shift between locations. Usually their range is between Location 2 and Location 4. Many do not consider later locations as 'better' than earlier ones, even though each further location seems to bring deeper levels of wellbeing with it. Instead, they realize that each location has its specific plusses and minuses for daily living.

For example, a Fluid 4 business owner and engineer might prefer to be at different locations depending on what is called for. Difficult engineering problems that can wear an individual down might be best worked on in Location 3. Business and financial decisions might be best taken in Location 2 or Location 4, depending upon their nature. The person's home life might be best supported by Location 2 or Location 3.

A Fluid 4 generally has access to each of these options, and is able to exert some influence over when they switch between them. Some can switch quite rapidly, especially if they have gained a lot of experience doing it. For most, it takes weeks, months, or even longer to move between locations. A Fluid 4 might not always be able to access locations that were experienced previously. Even a location that they have been in many times can go through periods, lasting from just a few moments to decades, where it is inaccessible.

Highly social individuals, or individuals whose jobs place importance on successful social interaction typically seek to move permanently from Location 4 back to earlier portions of the continuum. Although these individuals can become Fluid 4's, they often don't use that capability. Usually they just return to Location 2 or 3 and remain there. Sometimes later in life, they choose to advance to Location 4 again.

The other path that people take out of Location 4 involves moving further along the continuum. Location 4 provides a base from which to explore further. Location 5 and later locations are not covered in detail in this book, but they do exist and a small minority of people who reach Location 4 shift into them. For simplicity they are referred to collectively as Location 5+ or beyond Location 4.

LOCATION FLUIDITY

Although it is most common in Location 4, some Finders at earlier and later locations on the continuum also develop the ability to move between locations. A *Fluid 3* might be able to move between Locations 1, 2, and 3. A *Fluid 2* might move between Locations 1 and 2, although Finders who transition beyond Location 1 generally don't return to it even if they are Fluid. So, practically speaking, fluidity generally involves Locations 2 through 4.

Some Finders report having their home base become the "space" in which all of their previously accessible locations seem to exist. Although this most commonly only happens for a period of time, there are Finders who seem to lock it in and make it the persistent way they experience Fundamental Wellbeing. For these Finders, one of a few things becomes the case. Either they are able to shift their location consciously, their location seems to automatically shift to be what is optimal for the situation they are in, or some of each. There are Finders who argue that this is the "ultimate" form of Fundamental Wellbeing. They claim that it should develop to a point where the location being experienced in any given moment just naturally aligns with the situation one is in. Some liken this to the way an athlete trains to have actions be optimal and automatic for each moment while participating in their sport.

It was clear from the research that the individuals who made this case experienced different ranges and types of locations within Fundamental Wellbeing that they had access to. So, in order for their suppositions to be accurate only a specific subset of locations would be needed for each person's life.

It all doesn't come to a screeching halt at Location 4. Many more locations exist beyond these, and they can also be Fluid. *Fluid 5's*, for example, report that it is much more difficult for them to switch to Location 4 and earlier, though it can be done. There truly does seem to be a major chasm to cross in order to go back from these later locations. In fact, what lies at Location 5 and beyond will almost certainly astound you.

CHAPTER 14: LOCATION 5 AND BEYOND—THE FURTHER REACHES OF FUNDAMENTAL WELLBEING

Location 5+ refers to Finders who have arrived at Location 5 or later on the continuum. As mentioned, currently the project has not yet met anyone who initially transitioned to Fundamental Wellbeing beyond Location 4, though certainly it remains a possibility. As far as we know, everyone in the research so far moved to Location 5 or later after having been at Location 4, or another earlier location.

These further locations are an active area of research, and the project would love to hear from individuals who experience them. Although a full picture has not yet emerged, this chapter includes a bit of information about these locations, at a level that doesn't jeopardize the ongoing research involving them. Over the years, our policy has been to only provide information about an aspect of the research when we have finished with it. A minor exception is being made here because so many people ask about these later locations, and an increasing number of Finders seem to be experiencing the first few of them.

Many Finders almost immediately recognize Location 4 as an intermediary location in their journey. Others believe they have found the "final" location, and it takes them a while to realize there may be additional road ahead. For the Finders who have moved beyond it, Location 4 is most frequently described as the point where a great deal has been dissolved and disassembled, and a new level of opportunity created. Location 5 and later brings "reintegration" beyond anything that can previously be imagined. This includes very low-level brain processes such as dissolution and reassembly of how the senses are perceived, and even the reintroduction of emotions, for some.

THE DANGERS OF GOING TOO FAR, ALONE

The Finders who reach this portion of the continuum often realize that this isn't the first reintegration they've experienced. Some have traveled through every previous location, and looking back they can clearly see that each involved a reintegration, albeit less extreme than what is experienced in these later locations. At each location, the recontextualization of self and what came before results in a new way of experiencing life.

Each location from Location 5 onward generally involves at least one additional cycle of deep disassembly and reintegration. These seem to deal with scrubbing away the last vestiges of the Narrative-Self, and more. Unlike the previous locations, transition to these can be dangerous.

The pieces of the remaining aspects of the Narrative-Self that fall away in these later locations are often old, deep, and very complexly embedded in the psyche. Some deal with low-level processes such as how the senses come together to create experiences, and even fundamental body life support (breathing, heartbeat, etc.). Transitions in these later locations can cause temporary glitches in how these core systems function within the body. Fortunately, most often these disruptions are short lived and things reform quickly. However, when they take longer serious problems can result. They can even be life-threatening.

The research uncovered reports of individuals who remained unconscious, or who had serious difficulties with the function of their bodies for periods of days, weeks, and even longer after moving into one of these locations. Most of these individuals were in supportive social systems that cared for them during these times. Some, however, were not and seemed to be alive mostly from a stroke of luck. For example, they might have missed enough work that curious co-workers came looking for them, found them passed out on their living room floor, and called an ambulance.

The decision to move into these later locations is not to be made lightly. It's important to have sufficient social support and monitoring. This is tricky, because at Location 4 and beyond there is a tendency to want to isolate in order to go deeper and further along the continuum. The reason for this lies in the brain regions involved, and the impact that even rudimentary language use can have on the deepening process, versus silence. However, it is important to balance this with prudence, safety, and caution—no matter how certain one feels that everything will be okay.

THE FORK IN THE ROAD BEYOND LOCATION 4

Up to Location 4, the continuum is a single path. Things get more complicated at Location 5, and two different routes open up. The first, which will be referred to as the *Path of Freedom* (PoF), looks very much like a continuation of Location 4. The second one, the *Path of Humanity* (PoH), bears a greater resemblance to earlier locations. Generally speaking, the Path of Freedom was more common in Eastern research participants (especially monastics), and the Path of Humanity in Western ones.

Finders on the PoH often report a moment where it seemed like life could have gone down the other path, though some have buried this memory and do not become aware of it until asked. As part of learning that this other path exists, individuals on the PoH often report sensing aspects of the PoF as close, and identifying it as something they might be able to switch to. These types of intuitions are generally not reported by people on the PoF regarding the PoH.

The PoF involves many additional continuum locations when compared to the PoH. It's difficult to know how many, because the people who experience the furthest locations are so rare. Conversely, our project did not encounter PoH Finders beyond Location 9. The path selected may limit how much additional road a Finder can travel on.

Locations 5 through 9 seem to form a discrete set of locations, much as Locations 1 through 4 appear to. By the end of Location 9, when asked about their experience, regardless of path, Finders generally say something like, "it feels like it is just the universe looking out these eyes."

THE RETURN OF THE SELF

A number of longstanding religious and spiritual systems with an interest in the further reaches of Fundamental Wellbeing go to great lengths to warn people about how tricky the "self" can be. Anyone who has tried to reach Fundamental Wellbeing by meditating or using a similar practice will understand this warning. It's easy to feel like you're making progress, only to later discover that the Narrative-Self is in control, and has been fooling you and limiting your progress the entire time. During the early phases of the research project, we interpreted these warnings to be about this experience, which was often reported to us.

As the understanding grew regarding the PoF and the PoH, however, these warnings took on a new meaning. It became clear that the core processes in the brain that were responsible for constructing the Narrative-Self were also capable of constructing a wide variety of senses of self. Finders on the PoF seem to resist the pull of these brain mechanisms to a greater extent than those on the PoH. The Path of Humanity involves a subtle reconstitution of self that is often missed by those who are travelling on it. This self is very different from the Narrative-Self described elsewhere in this book, but may be one reason that these Finders appear to top out at Location 9. The limits this produces may also be why some systems stress the importance of keeping a vigilant watch out for the "self," regardless of how far you've progressed. This mechanism might also play a key role in another huge difference between the paths, as we'll see in the next section.

THE RETURN OF EMOTION

We tend to think that humans are born with a pre-defined range of emotional experience, and are all relatively the same. This is not the case. Consider the following example.

A child who is participating in a research project at the local university is lying on her bed when she hears a tone go off. The tone is coming from a pager she's been given that goes off at random times. When it goes off, she's supposed to open a diary and write down the contents of her consciousness from the exact moment it went off. She's undergone extensive training that makes this possible, and opens the diary to begin writing.

Later, she visits a researcher at the university who reviews her diary and asks questions to clarify what she wrote. When the researcher looks at the entry from that moment, she reads that the girl was lying on her bed, staring at the ceiling, thinking, "I'm so sad. I'm so sad…" A bit puzzled, the researcher says, "I see that you were lying on your bed, saying 'I'm so sad' to yourself. Were you also feeling sad but just forgot to write it down?"

The little girl replies, "No, I wasn't sad. I was just lying on my bed thinking, 'I'm so sad. I'm so sad.'" The researcher asks what was happening around that time, and the little girl tells her that the family had just finished watching a TV show that had made everyone she was watching it with very sad. So, she assumed that she must also be sad, and when she went to her room she was lying on her bed telling herself that she was sad, even though she wasn't actually feeling it.

This same research revealed that if we could fast forward a few years in this young girl's life, she would have learned to actually be sad in this situation. It has taught us that social situations train us how to feel, just as they train us how to think and act in so many other ways.

It's likely that there is a mechanism in the brain that is responsible for this form of learning, one that largely deactivates in Location 4 and stays inactive on the PoF, but that may remain active or reactivate on the PoH. The forms of emotion that disappear at Location 4 may primarily relate to the Narrative-Self, such as the types of socially constructed emotions from the example with the little girl. This brain mechanism may construct new forms of emotion for Finders in Location 5+ on the PoH, but base them instead on the building blocks found in those types of Fundamental Wellbeing, as well as the newly formed but very different and subtle sense of self found there.

One primary difference between the PoF and the PoH is that Finders on the PoH often describe a reintegration of and return to emotional experience. This is not the personal emotion that was present prior to Location 3 or 4. To some it can seem very much like aspects of traditional emotions, but impersonal. To others it can seem deconstructed. For example, a Finder might tell you that s/he loves you, but when asked what that really means, give an answer that sounds nothing like what the average person would consider love. Or, s/he might describe feeling God's love all the time, but when pressed for details, tell you that it is a feeling of energy in the lower abdomen that is there all the time and never stops flowing out into the world. We've collected countless different and highly variable examples.

In general, the subject of emotions from Location 4 on deserves its own book, and is far too complex to comprehensively cover here. However, knowing a bit about it and the PoH can make it easier to determine which path a Finder is on, so it's included here. The return of some degree of emotionality and this subtle, though usually overlooked, sense of self leads to Finders feeling more "human" again, thus the name Path of Humanity.

SENSORY CHANGES

Often, changes in the visual system seem to occur beginning around Location 5 and increase in intensity through Location 8. These can be foreshadowed in earlier locations. For example, some Location 4 individuals have reported shifts to two-dimensional instead of three-dimensional visions, but it is rare.

Given the large portion of the brain that is used for vision, these types of changes may represent more of it being co-opted by the deepening process. These visual changes can take many forms. Some individuals report having greater night vision, even to the point that darkness appears dim, but not actually dark. Relationships with light can also change, and objects can seem as if they are subtly self-illuminated in some way. This is especially true for things that aren't man-made, though for some it happens with everything.

As one progresses beyond Location 5, other visual and sensory changes can enter the mix. For example, a Finder may say that a statue of Christ, a Saint, a Hindu god, or the Buddha is moving, crying, speaking, singing, and so on—but be the only one present who can see or hear it. There have been a few times when multiple Finders from the same religious or spiritual tradition claimed to see identical things. Once, when a small group of Finders claimed that poetry was being recited by a statue of Buddha, I asked them to say what the statue was saying out loud as it was 'spoken.' They said the same words (in a language I was not familiar with) at the same time for several minutes. Of course, in situations like this there is no way to know whether they are playing a trick on me. They could have easily just been reciting a previously memorized text in sync. It is worth nothing, however, that a diverse range of individuals reports this type of phenomena.

INTUITION AND PSI

Locations 6 through 9 typically bring dramatically increased reports of accurate premonitions, intuition, and related experiences. For Finders, the degree this is the case differs based on whether someone is on the PoF or the PoH. Of course, these types of claims are always difficult to confirm, and it is worth noting that many people who do not experience Fundamental Wellbeing also report similar types of experiences.

For those on the PoF, these experiences appear to increasingly form a core part of their experience as a Finder. They are typically reported as both strengthening and increasing in intensity the closer one gets to Location 9. This also happens for individuals on the PoH, but is much less the case. It can be heightened for PoH Finders who seem to have innate capability in this area, work with special practices that seek such effects, and so on.

The closer a Finder gets to Location 9, the more reports of mind-matter interaction also appear. Typically, these are only glimpses, not things that can be brought about on demand. The scientific field that studies these types of reports is known as parapsychology. Parapsychological researchers refer to this phenomenon as *psychokinesis*, or *PK*. They have generally been interested in people that seem to be able to move things with their minds, manifest things they focus on, and so forth. Beyond Location 9, Finders report these types of experiences becoming more routine, and many regard them as a key feature of what appears in the next cluster of locations (roughly, Locations 10 through 21), much in the same way that things like accurate intuition become increasingly routine for those on the PoF in Locations 6 through 9.

As things like accurate intuition and PK are reported to enter the picture more routinely, Finders often have conditioning arise because these experiences conflict with their previous beliefs. In these later locations the conditioning typically dissolves rapidly, but it is interesting that this process occurs, because it suggests that at least some of these individuals did not previously believe these types of experiences were possible.

When asked what they make of these types of experiences, many Finders feel they are a logical extension of their direct experience. Think of it this way: a normal person believes they are their body because that is what they can feel, control the motor actions of, and so on. Finders in these later locations often feel that "they are the universe," not a being who is confined to a body. To them it makes perfect sense that, if this is true, they should be able to perceive as the entire universe. Thus, of course they should be able to know things without their body being present there. The universe is there, so they must be too. Likewise, just as someone can raise their arm, why shouldn't they be able to cause actions in the universe that are beyond their body, and what normal people would consider possible?

A range of interesting, publicly accessible first-hand stories about these types of events comes from an American named Lester Levenson (1909-1994). As a physicist, Levenson had been a die-hard physicalist and openly hostile skeptic towards these types of phenomena. After his own transition and deepening, he used those same skills to experiment extensively with it. Levenson openly made claims about calling people across the country and describing who was in the room and what they were doing, making objects move while others watched, using the abilities to become a millionaire in a short period of time (before giving it up because he realized he could manifest what he needed on demand), and so on. His stories, though increasingly hard to find since his passing, are remarkable and representative of views ones hears from Finders in these later locations.

It's good to keep a couple things in mind about these types of experiences. First, remember that many people report them who are not Finders. And, second, as we'll see in a later chapter, religious and spiritual traditions have often noticed these tendencies, and either encouraged adherents to move towards or away from them. At best, the scientific evidence in these areas seems conflicted and murky. However, there are some interesting examples from it that relate to Fundamental Wellbeing.

For instance, our project is aware of at least one individual who had the seeming ability to move physical objects in space correlate with his transition into Fundamental Wellbeing. It was the 1970's and the U.S. government was putting millions of dollars into funding rigorous scientific experiments into PK. This person participated in one such project, where eventually he learned to "dissolve his boundaries and merge with the experimental apparatus," and when he did so the target object would move and his state of consciousness would change. The experience of "dissolving his boundaries" led to him becoming a Finder. This case is interesting because it was a rigorous experiment, and also because the person did not initially land beyond Location 4 as a result of it, despite the fact that later locations are where these types of experiences are generally reported.

WHY ALL THE SECRETS?

One question that is always asked is, "Why aren't there more videos of this type of thing?" Perhaps the best answer is that, generally speaking, Finders at these later PoF locations just want to be left alone to continue their deepening into Fundamental Wellbeing. To some degree, their worst nightmare is people beating a path to their door over this or anything else. It took many years for the research project to build up a sufficient reputation for respecting confidentiality before individuals in these further locations were willing to speak to us, much less participate in the research.

As we saw previously, the seeds of this desire for increasing isolation begin in Location 4. When a Finder deepens in this location, it appears that key parts of their brain and its underlying networks that deal with symbolic thought and language undergo substantial change. Internally this can feel like something akin to a competition for energy in the brain. Imagine it feeling like you only have so much of this energy. When left alone to continue resting and deepening into Fundamental Wellbeing, this energy produces a profound sense of freedom and peace.

Conversely, it takes a great deal of this energy to produce what scientists call *theory of mind*. This means, in part, modeling another person's thoughts, feelings, and mind in general inside of yours in an effort to better understand and be able to communicate. For Location 4 Finders, it can feel like this takes even more of this energy to be able to process and understand speech, and formulate responses back in conversation. As you might imagine, that makes deepening in Fundamental Wellbeing far more desirable and rewarding than spending time with other people. Now imagine this continuing to deepen further at later PoF locations, and you begin to get a sense of how utterly undesirable it might be to have the world beat a path to your door.

In addition, later location PoF Finders have the sense that their form of consciousness is supporting the evolution of consciousness for all of humanity, and often much more. Internally it feels like their deepening on the continuum is widening a currently narrow path for others to increasingly be able to follow. If they go far enough, it may even feel like they are extending the path itself. This makes it seem much more important for them to keep going, rather than stop and try to explain what they are up to, or provide demonstrations they feel the world would be receptive to.

HOW FAR CAN YOU GO?

As you've already read, the position of the research project is that all locations have their own value, and that one is not 'better' than another. Just because some traditions seem to value the Path of Freedom and how far it can go, does not mean that the rest of us should accept their conclusions. Others feel the opposite, and our research suggests that a positive consensus opinion around the PoH seems to be forming in the West.

Certainly, it is possible to question the degree to which the transition to later PoF locations can even be supported in the average Westerner's life. The primary advocates for it come from Eastern monastic traditions, which have long-standing knowledge, methods, and social structures to support these types of transitions. Location 4 is sometimes said to feel "alien" by people who experience it. Those who transition to it from Location 3 often feel that they are coming out of the highest form of human development, into something else entirely. Sometimes the shift into Location 4 is downright shocking for Finders to experience.

From this perspective, the PoH offers an attractive alternative. Those on it generally feel that Location 4 was a transitional stage that allowed them to enter a much richer form of human experience. This is quite different than progressively more "alien"-like experiences that are often referred to by those on the PoF.

It is also important to keep in mind that it's likely not everyone can reach the furthest locations. Just as the capabilities of top athletes are a combination of innate ability and developed skill, the individuals who have made it to the furthest reaches of the continuum seemed to have built-in capabilities that facilitated it and were often foreshadowed since early childhood.

As with most forward shifts on the continuum, individuals at Location 5+ only rarely have a desire to return to Location 4. These further locations bring an even deeper wellbeing, sense of completeness, and so forth. When they do return, usually it is from the PoF and is typically out of a desire to be more effective in the world. The further PoF locations, though increasingly amazing, do not usually lead to increased skill in navigating society.

For those who are newly experiencing Fundamental Wellbeing, these seeming discrepancies can be a bit confusing. Just as with the example of fundamental okayness, these dichotomies are dealt with in many ways. Some are denied, others get explored, still others are tolerated, and so on. All of this is examined and sorted through in more detail in Part 4.

PART 3 – THE CORE ASPECTS OF FUNDAMENTAL WELLBEING

"The meaning of life is just to be alive.
It is so plain and so obvious and so simple.
And yet, everybody rushes around in a great panic as if it
were necessary to achieve something beyond themselves."
Alan Watts

CHAPTER 15: SENSE OF SELF

The most universal change reported by Finders relates to their internal sense of self, or what it feels like to be them. There are nuances within how a Finder's sense of self is experienced at different locations along the continuum.

Location 1 Finders experience a fundamental shift from the narrative-centered, highly individualized self that is common among non-Finders, to something that seems less personal, larger, and less isolated and separate. They often speak about a shift in the relationship with their body, and being less identified with and limited by it. They may also talk about feeling that they extend beyond their body, sometimes very far beyond it.

The shift to Location 1 can be very subtle, especially compared to the other locations. Unless they were depressed just prior to their transition, it's not uncommon for Location 1 Finders to just assume that something has occurred that lightened their load. They may not even realize they've moved onto the continuum until they transition to a later location. Nonetheless, there are clear signs if someone looks for them, as this section of the book will increasingly reveal.

Location 2 brings a more substantial change, and is much harder to miss. It involves a change from feeling like there is an ambiguous but definite center inside, to no center at all. For most people, the primary way of operating in the world comes from the perspective of this center, which feels like a locus of self. When they look out at the world, for example, they often feel as though there is a discrete center, or self, in them that is looking out at something separate from it. There appear to be two different things, the "looker" or "seer" (self) and what is being seen (what's outside of the self).

For Finders at Locations 2 and 4 (and, in most cases, beyond), this separate looker simply isn't there anymore and, more importantly, it isn't missed. In other words, it no longer feels like there is a strong, separate self that is looking out; there is only seeing. The looker appears to be unnecessary. Not only is the world often perceived as much more beautiful without it, but our experiments suggest visual perception can become both more comprehensive and accurate.

The same applies to other senses as well. Hearing, for example, usually involves a sense that there is an internal self that is listening. With the transition to Fundamental Wellbeing, in Locations 2, 4, and generally beyond, there is listening, but not the perception of a separate "listener" or "hearer." These are aspects of what is referred to as nonduality in some spiritual and religious traditions. The sense that the world is not comprised of self and other, and that there are "not two."

Location 3 is a bit different. Although Location 2 involves a form of nondual experience, Location 3 does not. Location 3 is found in many religious and spiritual traditions. In the Abrahamic traditions, it is the classic endpoint of their mystical traditions, where the spiritual adherent increasingly feels merged or unified with God. As you'll see later, Location 3 does not have this divine component for everyone, but here it provides a useful example. A Finder cannot feel merged with an outside force like 'God' if s/he is experiencing nondual perception, because the person would not have a sense of anything existing outside of him or herself to merge with.

So Location 3 is dual, but not in the same way as Location 1, or for non-Finders. The nature of self and other is much subtler in Location 3. In fact, it is so subtle that Finders who have transitioned from Location 2 to Location 3 often miss this change and assume they are still experiencing life from a nondual standpoint, until something causes them to scrutinize it.

A Location 3 Finder's sense of self feels very connected to both others, and the rest of the world in general. While a boundary can be found, generally a Finder has to look for it to see where the s/he leaves off and the world begins. There is a deep feeling of union and unity between the within and the without.

REMNANTS OF THE NARRATIVE-SELF

At most locations, some aspects of the Narrative-Self seem to remain, though Finders often aren't aware of it. It's possible that in some very far locations this is not the case, but the research on this is inconclusive at this point. Nonetheless, individuals at Location 2 and higher are likely to say that this sense of self has vanished, though there are things that can cast doubt on this for them.

First, especially at Locations 1 and 2, Finders are still able to be grabbed by streams of thought and pulled back into aspects of the Narrative-Self. This is much more common in Location 1 than Location 2. In Location 1, it can be so pronounced that some Location 1 Finders believe they are falling in and out of Fundamental Wellbeing when they aren't. There are aspects of this that can be useful for deepening that are discussed in Chapter 21.

Second, some Finders briefly experience aspects of, or even a full return, to their former self as a result of physiological processes like hypoglycemia or extreme fatigue. This can occur for individuals even up through Location 4. When this happens, it becomes clear that, at a minimum, significant aspects of the Narrative-Self are waiting in the background for their chance to reappear—and clearly have not evaporated forever.

Moving from one continuum location to another can also provide indications that a Finder's former sense of self might not be as purged as it seems. These shifts often involve previously unseen parts of the Narrative-Self falling away. The later the location, the more surprised a Finder often is to learn that unsuspected, hidden parts of their former sense of self have been lurking out of view.

It's also possible for Finders to realize this without shifting locations. Spiritual or religious practices, psychedelic drug use, extreme physical situations, illness, and many other things can provide a glimpse into a temporary state that reveals hidden, remaining aspects of their previous sense of self. Any of these can help a Finder to see that there may be even more shifts ahead, and accept that aspects of their Narrative-Self might still be present and exerting some unnoticed influence.

Finders also experience a huge change in their thoughts and thinking. In fact, many insist that all of their thoughts have "gone away." Many actually do.

CHAPTER 16: COGNITION

In addition to a core change in sense of self, Finders also experience a significant shift in the nature and quantity of their cognition (thoughts and thinking). This is typically among the first things noticed when they shift into Fundamental Wellbeing. From the outside, these changes can be hard to spot; consider the following paraphrase of a fairly typical conversation with a Location 4 research participant:

> *"So you're saying you have no thoughts?"*
> *"Yes. My mind is completely silent."*
> *"What is one plus one?"*
> *"Two."*
> *"Hmmm…Did you watch the presidential debate last night?"*
> *"Yes."*
> *"Do you have a favorite candidate?"*
> *"Usually I vote democrat, but I'm leaning towards the other person this time."*
> *"Why?"*
> *"I think his position on something I consider important is more in-line with my view."*
> *"But, again, you say you have no thoughts?"*
> *"Correct."*
> *"And no sense that there is an individual you?"*
> *"Right."*
> *"Hmmm…"*

It's easy to see how an exchange like this one can be somewhat baffling. It took a great deal of careful probing, experimentation, and analysis to unravel and come to grips with seemingly contradictory statements such as those in the example above.

The type and degree of changes in thoughts and thinking are related to a Finder's location on the continuum. Across the continuum, nearly everyone reports a significant reduction in, or even complete absence of, thoughts. However, a small percentage report just the opposite, that the quantity of their thoughts increases. Even when there are an increased number, the thoughts that remain exert much less influence than they did prior to Fundamental Wellbeing.

It's common for Finders to report that thoughts just come and go. They don't seem to have the same strong emotional charge they once did. They lack the power and saliency to "grab" or "pull" these individuals into the long thought streams and internal narratives where most others spend their day.

The degree of this differs for each of the continuum locations. The earlier the location, the more thoughts are still able to pull Finders into a Narrative-Self related thought stream. Generally, by the time a Finder has matured into Location 1, this is quickly noticed when it begins and the thought stream is released. This release happens much more automatically in Locations 2 and 3. By Location 4 the Narrative-Self related mind-wandering has reduced to almost nothing.

A SPECIFIC TYPE OF THOUGHT

Very early in the research it became clear that Finders were not actually referring to the disappearance of all thoughts. They remained fully able to use thought for problem solving and living an outwardly 'normal' life. In fact, they typically claimed that Fundamental Wellbeing shifted the mind to become a much more useful and powerful tool, "because it knows its place." Digging revealed that only a certain type had significantly changed: self-referential thought. This refers to thinking about one's self, and even more specifically the Narrative-Self thinking about itself.

Although they may not realize it, for non-Finders self-referential thoughts constitute a huge part of daily thinking. Even a simple request for the answer of 1+1 can bring a lot of self-referential thoughts with it, such as:

> *"Is this a trick? Will I look stupid if I get this wrong?"*
> *"I remember trying to divide those two candy bars among my three siblings when I was 12."*

And so on...

We rarely realize the degree to which these self-referential thoughts stick to and color other thoughts that don't have any need for them. When asked to quantify the amount of their thoughts that had vanished, Finders often cited 80-95%. When asked, none of them said they wanted their self-referential thoughts to return to previous levels, or to have their emotional charge return. On the contrary, they were quite grateful to be rid of both.

Given this high percentage, it's understandable why so many say their thoughts have completely fallen away. When this statistic is cited in public talks about the research, it's clear that most non-Finders believe it would be disastrous to lose 90% of their thoughts. This is hardly surprising, since most people are operating in the world through a narrative sense of self that is heavily linked to these self-referential thoughts, and their emotional content. Indeed, many assume that they *are* these thoughts.

Finders generally report that their problem-solving ability, and mental capacity and capability, have increased because they are not being crowded out or influenced by the noise of these missing thoughts. They describe their ability to think as more finely tuned, and as taking its appropriate place within their psychological architecture. "The mind is a wonderful servant, but a terrible master," sums up how many Finders feel about this change.

This change in cognition manifests in a variety of practical ways. During interaction with large or complex groups, whether at work or social events, Finders often feel like they are much more present than everyone else. They report being surprised at the quality of ideas that flow from their mouth, as well as the degree to which they can notice and deal with the transparency of others' personal, story-based agendas.

The shift can also bring a considerable degree of flexibility to interaction with others. Often, Finders' ability to communicate with very young children, people from other cultures, and so forth is enhanced. They routinely comment on how significantly this aspect of Fundamental Wellbeing has changed in their life for the better. Though they might not choose to take advantage of it, their mental liberation seems to provide them with much more cognitive flexibility for wide-ranging interactions, including ones that are far outside of others' comfort zones.

Changes in emotion often go hand-in-hand with changes in thought. The emotional differences that Finders experience are far-reaching, affecting their memories, perceptions, and more. These emotional changes seem to impact many parts of the Fundamental Wellbeing experience, and involve one of the most shocking changes that can occur.

CHAPTER 17: EMOTION

The emotional lives of Finders are very different than those of the average person. Just as they experience a reduction in Narrative-Self related thoughts, they also typically experience significant reductions in emotion. Depending on their location, this might mean a reduction in the amount of time some or all emotions are experienced, an absence of specific emotions, or a complete loss of all emotion.

In Location 1, Finders typically still have a full range of emotions. Personal love, anger, jealously, and other emotions are a regular occurrence in their lives, with two very notable differences. First, as mentioned in the previous chapter, a Finder who has matured into Location 1 or is in Location 2 will usually find the emotional content of their thoughts greatly reduced, making them less compelling. Second, emotions are less "sticky." Negative emotions don't linger as they tend to with non-Finders. They often only last a few moments, and can even arise and pass in a flash.

For many, getting cut off in traffic by a rude driver can produce a rush of anger. This is also true for many Finders. What happens next, though, differs remarkably. A non-Finder will often stay upset for varying degrees of time after the incident. We've all heard of the extreme forms of this, where resulting road rage leads to violence, but the milder forms are just as visible. For Finders, if emotion arises in a situation like this, it often passes quickly and is followed by a rapid return to equanimity. Why the difference?

One potential answer appears to be the lack of, or greatly diminished, Narrative-Self. For most people, emotions trigger or arise within a larger story. The narrative sense of self is tightly bound to these stories, and generates further actions based on them. What begins as a stimulus-response situation is prolonged by the stories and further actions that arise, all of which are quite literally 'self'-fueling.

Finders who experience emotions have a very different relationship to internal stories. While they can still get drawn into them, and other emotion-laden thought streams, these individuals are usually quick to realize it. Once they become aware of these thoughts, the stories behind them lose their power and typically just fall away. This deflates the reaction to the stimulus, and the emotional response it generated vanishes. The further a Finder's location is along the continuum, the less s/he is pulled in by stimulus-response, story, thoughts, and related influences.

In Location 1, and to a lesser extent Location 2, Finders might react strongly to the person who cuts them off. They may even demonstrate their feelings with a carefully chosen hand gesture. However, a moment or two later they will be calm. The stimulus and emotions linked to it arose, but there wasn't a sufficiently powerful Narrative-Self to latch on and extend the event with a story and its related emotions.

The distance Finders feel from emotion on these earlier portions of the continuum produces a strong and increasingly resilient experience of equanimity and wellbeing, but it is just the beginning of what's possible. As one progresses further down the continuum, triggered psychological conditioning increasingly causes less and less negative emotion to arise. Eventually all emotion falls away. Individuals at Location 4 who are cut off in traffic may experience a physiological response to alert them to a potentially dangerous situation, but no emotion arising along with it.

A CHANGING EMOTIONAL LANDSCAPE

As this suggests, the range of emotions Finders experience changes across the continuum. Between Locations 1 and 3, positive emotions such as love often increase, while negative emotions such as anger, jealousy, and hatred diminish. In a very real way, a person's baseline internal makeup changes for the positive with each step further along the continuum.

Finders at Locations 1 generally experience a full range of emotions. As mentioned, negative emotions fall off more rapidly, which leads to life seeming more positive in general. Location 2 is tilted considerably more towards positive emotion than Location 1. As Finders mature in Location 2, their emotional life becomes more and more positive, and they can reach a point where negative emotions are rare.

At Location 3, Finders typically only feel a single, positive emotion. It is usually described as a combination of other, formerly separate, positive emotions and feelings, such as: love, joy, compassion, and gratitude. I refer to these as facets of a single meta-emotion. Although this unified meta-emotion is the person's baseline, generally one or more of these facets is felt more strongly at any given time.

These facets, and the overall meta-emotion, are often experienced in an impersonal form. Rather than feeling like personal love, the love-based facet may feel like divine or universal love, or simply impersonal love. Despite this generalized sense, deep probing can often reveal that there are still some personalized aspects to these facets that go undetected by Finders.

How these facets are described can depend upon a Finder's belief system and ideology. For example, some Christians feel that "judgment" is a better descriptor than "compassion" for that facet of the emotion. When one really digs into how they mean judgment, surprisingly it looks very similar to what others describe as compassion. Christian and Islamic Finders are also more likely to feel the love facet as divine love.

Location 3 is usually, but not totally, devoid of negative emotion. If something major happens, such as the death of a beloved child, parent, or spouse, negative emotion can arise. Generally though, it takes an event of significant magnitude or the triggering of very deep and strong conditioning to make a dent in the continuous experience of Location 3's dominant meta-emotion.

As might be expected, because of this single multifaceted emotion, it feels amazing to live at Location 3. Finders who have experienced earlier locations often assume it must be the end, and many religions have viewed Location 3 this way as well. While there, it feels impossible to imagine what could be better. Ironically, all of this couldn't possibly be more different from the location that follows it.

At Location 4, Finders report an absence of emotion, but this doesn't mean they stop feeling great. Those who transition from an earlier location report a massive increase in both their wellbeing and sense of freedom. Given that Location 3 involved such a remarkably positive single meta-emotion, that the absence of emotion in Location 4 can feel even better seems surprising. These reports bring with them the peculiar suggestion that, far from being the source of wellbeing, even the most consistently positive emotion that we can imagine may not maximize our wellbeing.

Very few people seem to initially land, or subsequently transition into, Location 4. An example of one potential reason relates to personal love for one's child. Finders who have children often say that their transition to Location 4 didn't occur until they felt freed from the bulk of their parental obligations, whether by the death of their child or simply the child getting married and beginning a family of his or her (usually her) own.

Parents that experience Location 4 on the continuum lose their personal, individual love for their child. When asked, they often have redefined and recontextualized how they felt that love in the past. For example, they might say that they now realize that what they felt as deep parental love has been recognized as a nervous preoccupation.

On the surface, this might seem like a terrible sacrifice, and it can make one wonder what type of parent this produces. When asked about it, Finders seemed surprised at what resulted from this change. Each felt they had gained clarity and perspective that allowed them to be a much more present and effective parent than ever before. They seemed to have no doubt that this was a preferred form of consciousness to parent from, though they often did have concerns that their sense of this might be inaccurate, or that other parents might have concerns about their parenting style.

Though devoid of emotions, including seemingly essential ones like parental love, Location 4 Finders often still have experiences that the rest of us would probably describe as emotion. This includes experiences like felicity or frustration, though we must be careful here. How a non-Finder feels and experiences frustration is very different from how a Finder does, much less someone in Location 4. Nonetheless, it is important to note that there are aspects of the Location 4 experience that Finders describe that seem related to emotion, even though they would not call them that.

INNER PEACE

Regardless of what someone has heard about Fundamental Wellbeing, "inner peace" is almost guaranteed to have been at least part of the description. It is certainly true that participants at all locations reported levels of equanimity that can easily be referred to as inner peace. As with virtually everything else, there are nuances in how this shows up at various locations on the continuum.

In Locations 1 and 2, this feeling of equanimity can be temporarily, partially, and even heavily obscured. This seems to happen most frequently when a Finder's psychological conditioning is somehow triggered. It usually occurs when they are confronted with external circumstances and situations that cause them to react. This seems less frequently generated by internal triggers such as remembering a bad event from the past. The effects of this lessen the longer a Finder is within a location. It is also less pronounced generally at Location 2 versus Location 1. At locations further along the continuum, it takes increasingly more powerful and intense forms of conditioning, such as deep emotional patterns around serious family situations, for this to occur.

This suppression is usually described as the deep inner feeling of peace being "pushed down." When describing it, some will gesture with their hands, making a pushing down motion from their chest or solar plexus area to their lower abdomen. Finders also sometimes point to their upper chest, solar plexus, and / or lower abdomen when discussing their sense of peace. As with self-referential thoughts and emotions, this "pushing down" process diminishes and seems to only occur rarely, and in much less significant ways, at Location 4.

It's not uncommon for the suppression of this deep inner peace to involve a Finder's relationship with his or her parents, spouse, and children. Imagine this scenario: you are married to someone who has no interest whatsoever in Fundamental Wellbeing. Perhaps it even conflicts strongly with your spouse's most deeply held beliefs. You've been married for a number of years, and the recent years haven't been all that great. Your spouse knows from experience how to effectively 'push your buttons,' by triggering your conditioning and upsetting you.

Now, as a Finder, you've found deep, abiding inner peace. It's there all the time, except when you're with your spouse. When your spouse goes to the store, the deep peace wells back up. When your spouse comes home, the peace gets suppressed. How long would you stay in this relationship?

It is not uncommon for Finders in Location 1 and 2 to get separated or divorced in situations like this example. Others, particularly those at the higher locations, choose to stay in the relationship. The triggering seems to almost always extinguish over time. Committed relationships and Fundamental Wellbeing will be discussed more in Chapter 34.

The time frames uncovered in the research for extinguishing significant conditioning varied dramatically, but typically ranged from as little as two weeks to as long as seven years. The process is highly variable though, and even very strong conditioning can evaporate in a matter of moments. When the extinguishing takes longer than a few months, it's often because there are multiple layers of conditioning that need to be addressed. Like an onion, each layer of psychological triggers is peeled back from around a central core issue. For these most intense conditioned responses, the reactions involved with a layer most commonly extinguish within a couple of weeks to three months, and then the process repeats itself for the next layer of conditioning. For the most part this process feels automatic, and like it is just unfolding on its own.

It's very common for Finders in Locations 1 through 4 to report having at least one core issue that remains seemingly unresolved. They almost always know what it is. This was the case even though many years, even decades, had passed with the deconditioning process working away on it. Somewhat surprisingly, this also included individuals at Location 4. However, the way these Finders experienced triggers often felt quite different. They appeared as faint and vague sensations in the body, versus the very real diminishing of inner peace felt by Finders at earlier locations.

Other examples of both this pushing down effect, and deep triggers that don't seem to extinguish, involve long-term relationships. In one couple, the emotional trigger was so powerful and traumatic, and the extent of the pushing down so great, that it produced periods when the Finder no longer reported Fundamental Wellbeing. This is very unusual, as Finders typically describe the pushed down peace as suppressed but still present. When this person was away from the situation, Fundamental Wellbeing would return within two to four weeks. Like a yo-yo, it would disappear again when the interpersonal situation resumed. The Finder who reported this had previously been experiencing Fundamental Wellbeing for many years, and had experienced up through Location 4.

CONDITIONING AND THE SELF

Most people are familiar with the Russian psychology researcher Ivan Pavlov. He was an early pioneer in the research on psychological conditioning. His most famous research involved making dogs salivate when a bell was rung. It's a great example of how simple conditioning operates.

He gave food to the dogs, while ringing a bell. Soon, the dogs salivated when the bell rang because their nervous system assumed that food was coming. To 'extinguish' the conditioning, all he had to do was keep ringing the bell without presenting food. Eventually the dogs' nervous systems caught on and they stopped salivating when the bell rang.

Conditioning occurs for all of us in both simple and complex ways. From our research, we know that Finders can be conditioned just like everyone else. However, as the examples earlier in the chapter point out, it is possible for the conditioning that was accumulated prior to Fundamental Wellbeing to weaken or disappear altogether. It seems at least likely that the absence of the Narrative-Self is playing a role.

A significant amount or type of the conditioning people acquire over the course of their life relates to and is associated with the Narrative-Self. Just as many of our thoughts are self-referential, much of this conditioning may be as well. The reports from Finders make this seem likely. It appears that the Narrative-Self exists within a constructed, self-referential network of thoughts, emotions, memories, conditioning, and so forth. For at least some period of time, Finders seem to be going through life while the conditioning that was associated with their Narrative-Self gradually extinguishes. Of course, it is important to keep in mind that the body's condition-response system doesn't just switch off. New conditioning is always being created, though now from within the experience of Fundamental Wellbeing.

Some Finders experience traumatic transitions into Fundamental Wellbeing. It can be very psychologically and emotionally disturbing to have your experience of reality radically shift in such a short period of time. This can also occur when moving between locations on the continuum. These types of transitions can even involve periods of intense fear or depression. However, other strong cognitive, emotional, and even physical experiences have been reported.

These are familiar to many religious and spiritual traditions, which have assigned them names that range from the clinical sounding "de-stressing" to the terrifying "dark night of the soul." It seems possible that these might be especially intense extinguishing processes for batches of very deep, interrelated conditioning that are associated with the Narrative-Self. They can even occur in transitions between post-Location 4 areas on the continuum, as well as within Finders who have abided for some time in seemingly unshakably positive emotional states and high wellbeing.

Fundamental Wellbeing is strongly related to the way internal and external experiences do and do not trigger emotions and other reactions. Much of this relates to perception, and the way it changes with the introduction of Fundamental Wellbeing. Emotion is one thing, but can a heterosexual, Type-A male walk across a large university campus with bikini clad co-eds strewn about the rolling lawns, and not have attraction arise?

CHAPTER 18: PERCEPTION

On a warm day, walking across a large university's campus with one of my research participants, distractions lay in nearly every direction. At the time, this Finder was around Location 4 on the continuum, highly educated, and successful. We'd already spent several hours together, including a wonderful meal, and were now headed to get some local ice cream for dessert. As we walked across the manicured lawns, quite a number of beautiful young women were out sunbathing. Knowing that my participant was married and heterosexual, it seemed logical to ask if he was noticing them.

His answer was remarkable. "Occasionally my eyes will orient to and lock on one of them," he replied, "but nothing arises after that." When asked for more details, he matter-of-factly added, "I assume it is an instinctual procreation response deep in my physiology."

This incredibly straightforward answer remains among the best descriptions yet collected for what I call the *orientation response*. However, it didn't explain why he would orient to other things over the time we spent together, such as the traffic signal that was soon telling us when to walk. Even at Location 4, conditioning and learned behavior seem to still have their parts to play.

This core orientation response appears to be one of the fundamental building blocks of perception. Just as we saw with cognition and emotion, perceptual changes occur and grow more significant from location to location along the continuum, reaching a point similar to what is described above for Finders deep in Location 4. While the reaction of this participant was interesting, it was the behavior and responses of some Finders in Location 2 that were the most helpful in understanding the layers of experience involved with perception. They still had a range of emotions, and they were better able to perceive the finer details of them than individuals at Location 1.

Some of these Location 2 Finders reported that they could see how emotions unfolded in highly specific sequences. They could recognize the initial orientation response, followed by the physiological, cognitive, and emotional processes that arose next. This occurred even when there didn't seem to be a trigger in the environment. For example, at a very gross level, they might say that they felt a certain sensation occur in their body and knew a split second later anger would be arising, followed by thoughts that were related to the anger.

Although the lowest perceptual levels, such as the orientation response, seemed to be fixed, there didn't appear to be a universal order for how the higher-level layers arose. For some Finders, emotion came before thought. For others, the opposite was the case. Some were also much more in tune with their physiological sensations than others. The order reported could also depend on the type of initial orienting response.

Occasionally, participants could slice things into even more detail. For example, some could reach down far enough to report when the perception of linear time first entered their stream of consciousness. It's important to note that this ability to perceive a highly detailed range of perceptual layers, while helpful from a research standpoint, did not seem to be a core feature of Fundamental Wellbeing. The individuals who were able to do this were, most typically, accomplished meditators.

MANIPULATING PERCEPTUAL EXPERIENCE

Finders at Locations 2 and 3 often report reaching a point where some events are reacted to at one or more of these perceived layers, while other events are not. They are also more likely to be able to manipulate the overall process by effecting what's happening at current or arising layers. This was typically possible at Location 1 on a much grosser level, and generally not applicable at Location 4.

With the exception of ultra-low-level aspects such as the orientation response, most layers are reported as able to be manipulated. For example, an initial body sensation might signal when anger is about to arise. Some Finders can recognize this and actively dissipate it, preventing the follow-on emotion from arising. Even these layers and reactions can be sliced more finely.

An emotion can often be felt as a variety of components coming together to form it. I came to call these "proto-emotions," a term borrowed from a Finder who experienced them. These proto-emotions can also be consciously manipulated to prevent the full emotion from forming.

Using our previous example of getting upset when cut off in traffic, individuals who have this ability to perceive a finer level of detail and gain control over what layers arise also have more control over their reactions. Where someone at Location 1 on the continuum might have a short outburst and make a brief hand 'gesture,' individuals at Locations 2 and 3 usually have additional control. Depending upon their individual capability in this area, Finders may be able to choose to observe the orienting response, feel the physiological sensation or first inklings of thought that they know will soon bring anger, and consciously note it. From there, they can let the whole process go before anything further arises, or allow it to arise. Regardless of the choice made, it is a consciously observed event that can be manipulated in a highly specific way.

As one deepens in Location 2 and later, this process typically becomes increasingly automatic. Part of this simply relates to developing habits. If a Finder remains at the same location and keeps consciously using this to prevent undesirable thoughts and emotions from arising, the process will usually become habituated.

However, the further the location, the more automatic this process also seems to become. Individuals who initially land in Location 4 as their first experience of Fundamental Wellbeing generally report a great deal of automaticity, and obviously didn't develop it as a habit. For them, it was just something that happened. Finders at this further location typically report no sense of agency, meaning no ability to take action or make a decision. Life just seems to be unfolding.

Unresolved in all of this is what actions are defaulted to in this automatic mode. This goes back to that walk on the university campus, and it is a difficult question to answer. When you are with someone who reports no sense of agency or ability to make a decision, from the outside it can certainly seem like they are constantly taking actions and making decisions—such as where to go for ice cream. The reports of feeling this lack of agency are consistent across these Finders in Location 4, so we must accept that this is how it feels inside them, but what produces their actions remains a mystery.

How do the Finders explain this paradox? Typically, they say their best guess is that their behavior comes from some combination of genetics and biology, environment, and societal and cultural conditioning. The basic idea is that many things program their body and biologically based personality, and that somehow these come together to produce decisions and actions. It seems like a reasonable explanation. The second most common answer was simply, "God."

Going with the testable response, the research was able to determine that the combination of conditioning, biology, and so forth remains dynamic in Finders. Several experiments demonstrated that Finders at different locations on the continuum could be conditioned in a variety of ways. The system that is controlling their day-to-day lives and actions seems to take in new information and adapt in ways that are similar to the rest of the population. Of course, the key difference is that there is little to no Narrative-Self present to act as a filter, or additional step in the process. For the rest of the population, the Narrative-Self may make it feel like there is a greater sense of control.

Fundamental Wellbeing can bring unusual ways of perceiving the world along with it. For example, a tiny number of Finders experience a shift to 2-D vision. This can be persistent or temporary. When temporary, there are Finders who can intentionally bring it about, and others who just have it happen to them from time to time. Regardless of how it occurs, in this state the world seems to be moving through them, and not the other way around. Generally, this occurs at Location 4 and beyond.

THE PRESENT MOMENT

Another significant change that occurs in perception for Finders relates to their sense of time, and the present moment. In addition to inner peace, perhaps no other topic is as associated with Fundamental Wellbeing as living in "present-moment awareness," or simply the "present moment." Unsurprisingly, participants in the study reported a significant increase in their experience of, and effortless focus on, what was happening in the present moment, along with a dramatic reduction in thoughts about the past and future.

Over time the Narrative-Self learns that it can ignore a lot of what is going on in the present, and use that time in other ways. As a result, non-Finders often find their minds drifting to the past and future. Although the present moment is accompanied by seemingly endless sights, smells, sounds, and so forth, only a small percentage are noticed.

By contrast, a Finder's heightened present-moment awareness brings greater attention to sensory information. Looking at something doesn't mean ignoring smells or sounds. Information from all of the senses combines to produce a much richer experience of the present moment.

Some use this to detect when a thought stream is starting to grab them. They may notice, for example, that their sense of smell has diminished. They know that, for them, this is the first sense that drops off as they lose their present-moment focus. Noticing it weakening allows them to stay present.

Typically, the further along the continuum a Finder is located, the more reliably they are rooted in the present moment. Present moment focus has significant implications for memory, another key component that was studied. As with the other areas, the research uncovered substantial differences between those experiencing Fundamental Wellbeing and the rest of the population.

CHAPTER 19: MEMORY

The Finders' shift away from the Narrative-Self reduces the importance placed on their personal life history, or "story." This leads to less emphasis on their memories of the past. The extent to which this impacts an individual's memory is highly variable. As with the other core components of sense of self, cognition, emotion, and perception, the changes seem at least partially related to continuum location.

Memory is a complex area of study, and there are many types of it. This includes fact-based memory, memory that records your personal stories, memory that makes playing a sport or driving a car become routine, and short-term memory that flows through your brain and is quickly forgotten if not reinforced. Although the research to date has uncovered some interesting findings, there is undoubtedly much more to learn about the effects of Fundamental Wellbeing on the memory of Finders.

One of the most consistent effects involves memory and emotion. For virtually everyone, memories carry varying amounts of emotional charge. The strength of emotions linked to memories is greatly reduced in Finders. This charge fades even more the deeper they sink into their existing location, and the further they are along the continuum, until virtually no memories remain with emotional content.

One of the things long-time Finders often say that surprises people the most is that it "doesn't really matter" when someone transitions to Fundamental Wellbeing. Logic would dictate that the sooner in life someone can make the shift, the better—so why do they say this? The reason is simple: once a Finder has been in Fundamental Wellbeing for many years, the pain of the impact of their pre-Finder past recedes to the point that it doesn't seem like it was ever strong enough to be a concern. This is also why some are paradoxically heard saying that it doesn't matter if people even shift into Fundamental Wellbeing or not. They simply no longer remember what life was like before they were a Finder, so it doesn't seem like a big deal to become one.

Conversely, Finders who have recently transitioned often want those they care most about, and sometimes even everyone in general, to be able to experience Fundamental Wellbeing. This is especially the case if they were depressed, or even just unhappy prior to their transition. Some make dramatic life changes, choosing to write books or become religious or spiritual teachers, hoping to help others make the shift.

This zeal normally wears off as Fundamental Wellbeing becomes their new norm, which happens surprisingly quickly. Post-transition, there is an accelerated deconditioning process for Finders that lasts anywhere from a few months to a few years, with a couple years being the average. During this time, they adapt to their new way of experiencing the world so quickly that even they are often amazed by how soon it seems to become "nothing special." Not that they want to give it up!

One unintended consequence of this pattern is that many of the books, videos, and other materials produced, especially in the West, about Fundamental Wellbeing come from people who lived relatively unhappy lives prior to their transition. This colors their experience of how one reaches Fundamental Wellbeing, what locations are most desirable, and what it looks like on the other side. All of this, in turn, has significantly affected what many people have come to believe about Fundamental Wellbeing, norms in various religious and spiritual communities, and much more.

One unintended consequence of this is that these materials often make Fundamental Wellbeing seem terrifying to pursue for the average person. Tales of "dark nights of the soul" abound, the "disappearance of you" is stressed in a wide variety of ways, and worse. These two statements alone are enough to cause an ordinary person to run in the opposite direction.

Individuals spend their entire lives building up who they are. It's all they know, and it represents the foundation of stability in their world. Most certainly don't want to see it vanish in an instant. Notions like this conjure up a perilous journey with an uncertain fate at the end. Will someone be able to work, or will they be like the spiritual teachers who talk about being non-functional for years after their transition?

What will become of their family and other relationships? Who will pay the mortgage, put their kids through school, and so on?

Ironically, the authors and teachers who produce these materials rarely think about this. They were all too happy to "lose themselves." The disappearance of the Narrative-Self that had been torturing them for so much of their life was the greatest thing that ever happened to them. They want everyone to know it's possible, which is why they often become Fundamental Wellbeing's strongest advocates.

Unfortunately, this has probably driven more people away from Fundamental Wellbeing than drawn them towards it. From the research we know that these once tortured souls represent a tiny fraction of those who become Finders. Most 'ordinary' people transition, and simply go on with their lives. Their world does not fall apart. On the contrary, they get all the benefits of their former lives plus those associated with Fundamental Wellbeing—an ultimate win-win scenario.

The downside of this win-win in Finders' lives is that it means they only rarely stop what they are doing to advocate for and share their experience of Fundamental Wellbeing, which leads to a lopsided perception of it in the public's eyes. If more of the 'average' Finders did this, the rest of the population would most likely realize that Fundamental Wellbeing is what they've been looking for their entire lives. It's what allows advertisers to convince them that the next car, house, shirt or snack will get them one step closer to happiness, peace, and contentment. They'd be able to understand that Fundamental Wellbeing addresses their core discontentment in a way no product, relationship, job, or life circumstance can—by making it go away entirely.

EMOTIONS AND MEMORY

Finders' emotional content varies. Despite their reduced charge in Location 1, memories still have a mix of positive and negative emotions associated with them. By Location 3, even 'bad' memories are often biased towards positive emotion.

Both encoding (storing) and recalling information can be affected by Fundamental Wellbeing. Even though much less importance is placed on personal memories, on the early end of the continuum changes in encoding are generally not reported. In other words, these early location Finders feel that what they store in memory is essentially the same as before their transition.

However, they also state that personal memories seem to spontaneously arise less than they did previously. This reduction in memories coming to mind as thoughts seems to increase the further a Finder is along the continuum. This makes sense within the overall picture that emerged during the research.

For the average person, autobiographical memories often come to mind alongside self-referential thoughts. As we've discussed, this type of thought is reduced in Finders, so it's not surprising that they have fewer spontaneous memories arise about their past. Autobiographical memories lie at the very heart of the story-driven Narrative-Self, and its increasing reduction or absence seems to bring these memories to mind less and less.

Going from an internal landscape that is heavily populated by these types of memories to one that is devoid of them can lead Finders to assume they are losing their memories. As a result, some Finders at every stage on the continuum say that they have "poor memories." However, the research performed with these individuals generally did not confirm their view.

Even anecdotally, when digging deeply into their past during interviews or casual conversations, in almost all cases their memories seemed both highly accessible and comprehensive. They had plenty of access to information that they had accumulated over time. And certainly they didn't lose the ability to drive a car without needing to be fully mentally engaged in it, or to dress and feed themselves.

Further along the continuum, Finders are more likely to report difficulty with encoding memories of the events that comprise their days. Again, while this is their perception, it does not appear to be entirely the case. They are typically rich sources of personal history. Long-term research participants seemed able to seamlessly recall events from earlier times we spent together. Initially, their perceived memory loss, or lack of encoding, seemed to primarily be an illusion created by the further reduction in or absence of the self-referential thoughts that brought memories to mind prior to Fundamental Wellbeing.

Over time, however, it became clear that Finders often don't store some things in memory as well as others in the general population. These are easy to guess based on what is known about Fundamental Wellbeing. For example, Finders often have a reduced interest in stories, and perhaps unsurprisingly, some cannot recall the details of many of the movies they've watched or books they've read that are story-based. In some instances, they can't even remember which titles they have or haven't consumed. This is an area where much more research is needed to tease out all the details of what is and isn't changing.

THE NEED FOR LISTS

There is one noticeable memory issue that seems to be a reliable and genuine deficit. While most common with Location 4 and later Finders, this issue can manifest at earlier locations, especially if someone has deepened significantly into Location 2 or 3. These individuals report that they are often unable to remember planned events and scheduled appointments that are not part of a routine. For example, they might consistently remember to pick their child up at school each day, but forget irregular appointments such as doctor visits. Although rare, it can also occasionally affect routine events, including very basic life tasks such as remembering to brush their teeth, if these types of things are not done at a fixed time each day.

The Finders who experience this typically adapt their routines to adjust. Many immediately add scheduled events to a list as they are making plans. They display these lists in places around their house or car where they're most likely to be noticed, or adopt a regular routine for checking them. It was not uncommon for these individuals to tell me that they only remembered I was coming because they happened to glance at a list close to the time we were scheduled to meet.

When we visited their homes, these lists could often be found stuck to televisions, computer monitors, bathroom mirrors, refrigerators, purses, and doors that lead to the garage or outside. It was clear that these lists were consciously being placed in locations that the Finder would look with at least some degree of regularity as they went about their day. As the years have passed and smart phones have become more widely used, Finders have increasingly adapted to using the sophisticated calendar systems and list-making applications they contain to help solve this issue.

At this point, the primary transformations that underpin Fundamental Wellbeing have been covered. These include the core shift in sense of self, as well as the major changes in cognition, emotion, perception, and memory. We've started to glimpse what it feels like to be a Finder. Fundamental Wellbeing is so different from the 'normal' way that most people experience life, it can be hard to grasp. The next chapter fills in some of the major missing pieces and provides an even more complete picture of what it is like to experience the world from this extraordinary perspective.

CHAPTER 20: OTHER KEY ASPECTS OF FUNDAMENTAL WELLBEING

Many Finders experience a rapid and immediate shift into Fundamental Wellbeing, and one of the closest similarities to it is being awakened from sleep in the middle of a dream. Because of this, some Finders use the term "awakening" to describe their transition. Early in the research it became clear that words like this were not simply meant as metaphors, even though that is often how they are interpreted. When Finders use words like awakening, they are often trying to select the closest and most precise word they can find in language to describe their actual experience.

Of course, a key difference between Fundamental Wellbeing and waking up from a dream is that the world being experienced is persistent. They are still in the same room, park, car, temple, stadium, or wherever their awakening occurred. It's common for them to say things like, "nothing changed, but nothing is the same," or "everything changed, yet it is still the same."

These types of phrases can be confusing, and it helps to realize that this is a literal attempt to describe what happened. The physical world around them, in most cases, did not change. Yet, the experience of it, and how it is perceived and related to, did. Sometimes this change can be very subtle, other times it is overwhelmingly dramatic.

Once the perspective of the Narrative-Self is removed, it no longer colors how the world is experienced. At least it appears that way to Finders. Recall that although it seems to be gone at each location, our research suggests that more of the Narrative-Self is uncovered and falls away with each later location on the continuum, at least up to a point. This can also happen when Finders sink deeper into their existing location.

After their transition, it is very common for Finders to say that they realize their Narrative-Self was never real at all. This is especially true beyond Location 1. For those who don't experience Fundamental Wellbeing, a statement like this can sound, well, crazy. This is one reason why so many Finders don't disclose what is going on inside them. At best, they don't want to worry their friends and family. At worst, they don't want to have to fight to prove their sanity.

It is also common to hear a Finder talking about experiencing "reality" or the "real world" for the "very first time." This refers to experiencing the world as no longer colored by the Narrative-Self. From the new viewpoint of Fundamental Wellbeing, especially from Location 2 on, it appears as if the previous sense of self was nothing more than a story that's no longer relevant. Now, the Narrative-Self and the way it colored the world both seem gone, or at least significantly reduced.

Some Finders use the phrase "die before you die" to refer to the disappearance of the Narrative-Self. Occasionally, the moments before the transition to Fundamental Wellbeing can be as terrifying as accepting physical death. It can feel like a psychological death, yet the only thing that seems to actually leave is the Narrative-Self. The body and all its senses, the life animating it, the person's memory and personality, and so forth remain.

The Narrative-Self seems to be the part of us that fears and obsesses about death. Fear of death is one of the things that fades away for most when Fundamental Wellbeing arrives. This doesn't mean that Finders no longer care if they live or die. Rather, the fear of death often leaves, and brings a tremendous feeling of liberation with it. Life is still cherished, but death is not feared.

In fact, many fears and anxieties diminish or leave altogether with the Narrative-Self. It seems that its obsession over the past and future, dogged pursuit of validation, and never-ending problem finding suppresses our innate peace and wellbeing. Unless someone is in immediate physical danger, in all likelihood the only threats to wellbeing are coming from thoughts about the past and future. In Finders, the reduction or absence of these thoughts allows a peaceful and positive internal state to arise.

FILLING THE "GOD-SIZED" HOLE

Another remarkable thing that arrives with Fundamental Wellbeing is a sense of completeness. Religions commonly use the phrase "God-sized hole" to describe the sense of an internal void most people feel. This is powerful recruiting language, as even happy people typically realize they feel incomplete. A famous advertising executive once said, "We're never going to make a commercial that says you're okay, exactly as you are." The entire marketing industry thrives on pointing out this hole and the persistent underlying sense of discontentment that everyone has in them, and then trying to convince them a product or service will fill it.

Of course, the hole never gets filled. While having a great marriage, a wonderful family, amazing relationships, enough money, and spending your life in meaningful pursuits have been shown to increase happiness and wellbeing, ultimately even these are not able to fill that God-sized hole. Most people live their lives in the constant pursuit of what will fill this void, whether they realize it or not.

They listen to their thoughts about what might fill the hole, pursue those things, and get at least some of them. Of course, no amount of success fills the hole and the process repeats. Sound familiar? Ironically, the most successful people among us, those who achieve their goals again and again, often come to believe that their hole simply cannot be filled. Nothing could be further from the truth.

Fundamental Wellbeing fills the hole. More correctly, it produces the realization that there never was a hole at all. The hole related to the Narrative-Self, which is now recognized as just an old and powerful collection of thoughts that was never 'real' in the first place. The feeling of a 'hole' was simply the Narrative-Self endlessly trying to cover up that secret. With that realized, the deep feeling of having a hole goes away, along with fear, anxiety, discontentment, and a host of other things that accompanied it and won't be missed. Finders seem to be the only people who truly have their seeking and hole-filling come to an end.

You might be wondering at this point what comes after Finding. The answer is exploring and simply being. In a very real sense, people go from seekers to Finders and then on to explorers. Simply being in existence is amazing, and there's no shortage of it to explore. Doing that from peace rather than a compulsive underlying sense of discontentment brings a life beyond compare.

GOALS AND MOTIVATION

The average person's goals are driven in part by the desire to fill the God-sized hole. With this need gone, goals are one of the things that can significantly change for new Finders. To some degree, the extent of the change depends on where a person is on the continuum.

Finders in Location 1 and the early portions of Location 2 have higher amounts of agency and conditioned behavior. At these locations, even very materialistic goals, such as still wanting a certain car, remain fairly common just after the transition. However, these Finders typically notice that they are no longer willing to make the same degree of sacrifice to achieve these types of goals.

This is also true for Finders who are climbing the organizational ladder at work. Each step up that was considered so critical in providing further credibility and status to their Narrative-Self becomes less important. This does not mean their performance at work suffers. Finders often feel that it significantly improves.

By the later portions of Location 2, and into Location 3, reductions in both conditioning and the importance of outcomes make goal attainment increasingly less pertinent. At Location 4, life seems to simply be unfolding, and it feels like there is no need or ability to take action or make decisions. In this location, goals don't seem especially relevant, though things continue to get done.

One issue that can occur at any location on the continuum for new Finders is a lack of motivation. Most people spend their entire lives pursuing various directions that they think are most likely to give them what they want. The underlying motivation for all of this comes from the Narrative-Self and its stories. When it diminishes or goes away, their motivation structure dramatically changes.

Up to that point, a tremendous amount of wiring in their brain has been built up in the direction of those desires, and the motivations behind them. Becoming a Finder often pulls the rug out from underneath all this. The end result can be a loss of motivation that can last from a few months to over two years.

If you've read the book up to this point and not skipped around, this time frame should sound familiar. It's the same as the initial deconditioning process that typically follows the transition to Fundamental Wellbeing. Many things are taking place during this period, and this is one of the most important.

What seems to be happening is a recalibration in the brain. Old neuronal connections that were involved in a Finder's previous motivations are atrophying, and new ones are beginning to emerge. The old ones are so deep and pervasive that the process takes time to complete. When it does, new motivations seem to bubble up out of nowhere. Interestingly, these can support long-standing goals and preferences, or generate entirely new ones. This seems to relate to how "on path" they were in the first place. Finders who aren't especially aligned with their job and life are most likely to have new goals enter, and to take a new direction in life.

These first two years of Fundamental Wellbeing are a critical time for new Finders. Their path for the first seven or so years of the experience seems to be established during this time. They can exit the process as a highly effective member of society, or living in their kid's basement, depending on how it goes. The good news is that the process is highly malleable and can easily be directed towards an optimum outcome.

APPROVAL FROM OTHERS

A great deal of human social interaction is built around seeking and granting approval. Once the God-sized hole is filled, the need for approval changes. Like so many things, how this shows up depends on a person's location on the continuum. Although it is progressively lessened over Locations 1 through 3, seeking approval exists in some form right up to Location 4.

Location 1 Finders typically seem completely 'normal' in social interactions. Internally, they now realize that self-referential stories underpin most social interaction, and they are probably struggling a bit with their reduced interest in these narratives. However, they have enough conditioning remaining to ensure that this disinterest isn't especially visible, and they are still highly functional socially.

This lessens at Location 2, though Finders at this location remain socially adept. There is one significant glitch that can occur. A temporary phase may be experienced when approval is virtually unimportant. This seems to happen when a certain type of conditioning is working its way out. Location 2 Finders experiencing this can seem atypically antisocial and rude during this period.

Although individuals at Location 3 have even less need for approval, their loving and caring demeanor covers this up and provides plenty of approval from those around them. By this location, Finders often feel a strong disconnection from social norms. They have very little interest in the stories that underpin social relationships. At the same time, they see the practical value in playing along because of the connection it gives them to others, which in turn allows them to be of greater service. They are also aware of how much approval matters to non-Finders, and their caring nature takes this into account when interacting with them.

Over time, Finders at Location 4 extinguish virtually all conditioning around approval. This provides them with an immense sense of freedom, but also an increasingly significant handicap in social situations and relationship building. They are often able to form short- and mid-term length relationships, but longer and deeper ones with non-Finders present more of a challenge. Mental and emotional support for non-Finders typically comes down to listening to, empathizing with, and supporting the seemingly endless personal stories their Narrative-Self wants to tell about itself. Location 4 Finders simply have no interest in investing significant amounts of time doing that.

These individuals are rarely aware of the degree to which this impacts their social life and connection to others. They often feel that they have much stronger social bonds than is actually the case. On the other hand, they feel complete and have a deep sense of freedom and wellbeing, so they typically don't care.

This may seem at odds with the previous statement about Location 4 Finders feeling more at ease in communicating across a wide variety of people. The difference is one of degree. Their increased sense of freedom from approval and intense present-moment awareness can give them a very broad range of interpersonal communication skills. However, if a person has been in Location 4 for a while, that same freedom from approval, the elimination of conditioning around social norms, and other key elements of this location often make it hard to establish longer-term and more meaningful relationships.

SILENCE, STILLNESS, AND SPACIOUSNESS

The departure of the Narrative-Self and the reduction in self-referential thought that comes with it, can bring on a profound sense of internal silence, and a corresponding sense of internal stillness. Most non-Finders experience an ongoing buzz of thoughts, emotions, and memories. They are used to this drone of activity and consider it perfectly normal. Until they experience a moment without it, it's impossible to realize the extent of the impact it is having on their lives.

Among groups that seek to quiet their minds with contemplative prayer, meditation, or similar methods, it's not uncommon to encounter phrases like "the motion of thought" or "the movement of thought." The same is true for Finders. When you silence your mind sufficiently, thought can clearly be sensed as "movement" in the mind. The sense of movement produced by thoughts can be so strong that it can even make it feel like someone has been off exploring distant times and places, when s/he has really only been sitting or lying still.

With Fundamental Wellbeing, an underlying silence and stillness can remain detectable for Finders who have deepened significantly, even when experiencing the few thoughts, emotions, memories, and so forth that remain. In fact, silence and stillness can seem like they infuse and lie at the very heart of even the experience of thinking.

Along with this silence and stillness, Finders also commonly experience a deep sense of spaciousness. Think of it this way: something must be aware of all those thoughts, emotions, and memories. Imagine that you've spent your whole life stuck in a theatre watching one endless movie. Worse yet, that there is a thin, mostly transparent curtain covering the screen that is subtly moving from the climate control vents blowing on it, yet assume that you are seeing the picture clearly.

All of a sudden, the thin curtain opens and you can clearly see the movie; then the movie stops, and the blank screen it was projected upon comes into view. You now realize that all this time there was a 'space' that contained the movie's moving images but was unaffected by them. Not only weren't you aware of it, you weren't even aware of many of the movie's details.

This is, of course, a bit too simple of a metaphor because the screen cannot perceive the movie. And the reality of the human experience is that a fundamental level of our awareness appears to not only be acting as the screen, but also the projector, movie, light, and sound. Everything seems to be appearing within this totality of awareness.

There appears to be something that contains and perceives thoughts, emotions, information from our senses, and even our sense of self. A perception that is always on when we are aware. Fundamental Wellbeing pulls this awareness from its hidden background location into view. The shift of perspective this causes is central to much of what a Finder experiences.

AGENCY

Agency, in this book, refers to the ability to take actions and make decisions. If you believe that you can stop reading this book right now, you have a sense of agency. It has most likely been with you for as long as you can remember, and probably feels like an unchangeable and fundamental building block of who you are. One of the surprising things about Fundamental Wellbeing is the changes that occur involving it.

Location 4 Finders say they do not have a sense of agency. Individuals at Locations 2 and 3 can also comment that, "there is no doer." This is related to the earlier discussion of there being no "seer" (or "hearer," etc.). It seems to imply a lack of agency, yet these Finders are often turned off when they hear about the absence of emotion and agency in Location 4. So, what's going on here?

"No doer" in earlier locations on the continuum typically refers to the perceived weakening and increasing absence of a Narrative-Self. This form of self views itself as "the doer," even though it often isn't. If that seems like a bold claim, ask yourself how much 'you' feel responsible for your health. Non-Finders generally feel very responsible for it. Their sense is that they are making decisions and taking all kinds of actions every day to protect their bodies.

However, there are untold numbers of processes happening in trillions of cells right now to keep them healthy. Given this vast scale, there is simply no way people can be consciously in control of what most of these cells are doing. There is also an atmosphere that is sustaining life on the planet, law enforcement keeping them safe, and so forth. The percentage of their health that they actually control is incredibly small compared to the portion they don't control. Despite this, their Narrative-Self feels that it is in control and taking good (or maybe not so good) care of them. That's the doer.

With Fundamental Wellbeing, this "doer" increasingly disappears. Finders still make decisions and take actions, but how it feels changes. And, it is different across locations. In Locations 1 through 3, it can certainly feel like there is involvement in decision-making and taking action, just not always as "the doer." At Location 4, even this sense goes away.

BODY AND MENTAL CONDITIONS

Fundamental Wellbeing can impact behavior involving addictions at all continuum locations. Some Finders say that their transition cured their alcoholism or drug abuse. Paradoxically, however, plenty of other Finders remain alcoholics or drug addicts, smoke, and/or engage in similar types of activities.

These individuals aren't especially helpful in explaining their behavior, and often describe it as "just happening" or "what the body wants." When asked about the impact on their body's health, they often give answers that seem quite dissociated from it, or point to having no fear of death. For the most part, many of these individuals genuinely do not appear concerned with the potential health consequences of their actions and addictions.

On a related note, while Fundamental Wellbeing generally doesn't cure people's illnesses, it can have positive health effects. Finders who lived with intense chronic pain prior to Fundamental Wellbeing are often surprised by how it lessens. According to them, the Narrative-Self's stories magnify and extend the underlying physical pain. With this sense of self weakened or out of the way, the experience of pain fundamentally changes, and is reduced.

A small number of Finders experience a deep bliss sensation all through their body, including during moments that would otherwise be physically painful. For some, this seems to bring pain tolerances that appear infinite. A few of these Finders have reported experiences that should have involved horrific amounts of pain, but only resulted in bliss. Others who experience ongoing bliss find that they can reach its limits. They report a threshold, unique to each individual, above which pain is experienced.

Fundamental Wellbeing can also take away the psychological suffering associated with illness, but not the physiological condition itself. For example, there are Finders who experienced intense anxiety and physical tremors prior to Fundamental Wellbeing. The shaking and anxiety felt like they were part of the same condition. After their transition, they lost the anxiety but needed to continue to take their medication to prevent the tremors.

EMBODIMENT

A commonly used word among some Finders is *embodiment*. It is generally used to refer to "embodied" forms of Fundamental Wellbeing. Because the phrase is used in a wide variety of ways it can be a bit difficult to nail it down. However, in general there are two high-level ways it is used. The first way refers to the deconditioning process. People who use the term typically view some forms of Fundamental Wellbeing as primarily being "in the head," or conscious awareness focused. This, they argue, misses the rest of the body.

Certainly it seems true that a great deal of our psychological conditioning is tied to the body. For example, when a traumatic event happens, the mind can associate a wide range of stimuli with it, such as the moment's sights and sounds. It can also associate body-specific conditions with it, such as the symptoms of an illness, the position of one or more body part, whether you were out of breath, and an almost endless number more.

Much of the psychological science of *behaviorism* deals with addressing conditioning though its various awareness (i.e., light, sound, touch, taste, and smell) and body-based (i.e., illness symptoms) associations. These same methods can be used to eliminate psychological conditioning that allows one to deepen into Fundamental Wellbeing. The body-based ones relate to this form of embodiment.

The second way this term is often used is a bit more esoteric. It deals with a belief in specific types of "energies" and "energy flows" that are said to occur in or around the body. Science hasn't made much progress in detecting and measuring these, but the individuals who believe in them swear that they are real, and extensively mapped out.

This version of embodiment involves the use of these energies to enhance Fundamental Wellbeing. The gist is that by becoming aware of these various energies and doing certain things with them, such as moving them around the body in specific ways or amplifying them, it creates more capacity for, or even directly charges up a person's physiology with, Fundamental Wellbeing. In this sense, by becoming more embodied, it is believed a person can more fully and deeply experience Fundamental Wellbeing.

RACISM AND SEXISM

Finders can be racist and sexist. The project explored this early in the research, when some participants claimed to be free from these types of bias. When tested with the physiological-based tests from Harvard's Project Implicit, the results typically showed average amounts of racism and sexism, regardless of continuum location. This often surprised the participants involved, who genuinely felt that these dispositions had left with their Narrative-Self.

It's unclear if this test revealed remaining conditioning that was stored in their bodies, or deeper, hidden psychological biases that weren't consciously accessible. Both carry the same implication, that unconscious tendencies can still affect real world actions. Because of their hidden nature, Finders often don't have much if any motivation to work on or correct these types of inclinations, a topic we explore next.

CHAPTER 21: ZOOMING-IN AND ZOOMING-OUT

How we feel when relaxed (*zoomed-out*) is very different from how we feel when focused and working on something, or engrossed in a movie (*zoomed-in*). This is true regardless of whether or not we are a Finder, but some significant differences arrive with Fundamental Wellbeing.

Although it's not the typical experience, when the average person is hyper-focused the influence of the Narrative-Self can be minimized. Athletes, artists, mathematicians, and others refer to this as the "flow state" or being "in the zone." It is also possible to experience this when absorbed in a story, such as a good book or movie. When these moments of hyper-focus pass and awareness zooms back out, the Narrative-Self re-exerts its influence. This might lead to thinking about tasks that need to be completed, a conversation from three hours ago, or any number of other things.

Finders have a much greater range and fluidity when it comes to *zooming-in* and *zooming-out*. At the furthest reaches of zooming-out, some refer to being immersed in, or existing as, undifferentiated spaciousness or awareness. Union with and being indistinguishable from "all that is," the Universe, the divine, or God, is another common report. When zoomed this far out, a Finder typically cannot interact with the world around them. Not all Finders can zoom this far out and, for obvious reasons, those who can usually stop short of it in their day-to-day lives.

The zooming-in process is also different for Finders, but in some ways they are typical of the rest of the population. Many can still 'lose themselves' in a movie, for example. Nonetheless, there are striking differences that point to what is one of the least known and talked about aspects of Fundamental Wellbeing.

Some Finders are able to experience "versions" or "pieces" of their former Narrative-Self as part of the zooming-in process. This is especially true when they are engaged in conversation. Just silently hanging out

119

with someone that they have a long and complex relationship with can also produce it. These Finders often describe this experience as being triggered by the types of conditioning discussed previously.

These pieces of their former Narrative-Self show up internally as clusters of related thoughts, emotions, and memories. We'll call these *Narrative-Self clusters*. Each is felt to have distinctive aspects of a narrative sense of self associated with it.

In much the same way that most people can identify with a character in a movie, these Finders can zoom in to a cluster and immerse themselves in its unique sense of self, then zoom back out again. Essentially, this is like temporarily putting on the cluster, assuming aspects of its personality, and so forth. Some have a great deal of control over how far they zoom and the degree to which a cluster can grab them and pull them in. Others experience the process as automatic. Most experience a mix between these two.

A range of triggers seems to be able to initiate the automatic zooming process, including: language, conditioning, external stimuli, and becoming aware of a thought stream. For those with conscious control of the zooming process, in a given situation they can choose how far they want to remain zoomed-in or -out.

'SELF' IMPROVEMENT

Many Finders were self-help junkies prior to Fundamental Wellbeing. After the transition, their newfound sense of completeness can dampen this behavior. They are no longer searching for fixes or improvements. It doesn't help that most self-help methods are designed to work on the Narrative-Self, making them seem like a waste of time to Finders.

However, from a social or health standpoint, this can be detrimental. For example, as mentioned earlier Finders can still be sexist and racist. Latent conditioning and unconscious mental processes like these can be useful to work on. We also saw that Finders can remain addicted to smoking, alcohol, and drugs. Obviously, these have very real health consequences.

Many Finders still have to earn an income, raise a family, and engage in other important social roles. The lack of social polish that arrives as a Finder deepens in Location 4 can be detrimental to these unless properly addressed, yet the shift doesn't make changing these types of behaviors a priority.

Some Finders are an exception to this. They choose to continue trying to adjust their "programming," and the Narrative-Self clusters are where they've discovered modifications can be made. For example, in a social situation these Finders will use a carefully chosen amount of zoomed-in depth, or the automatic level experienced, to make changes. They focus on and engage with the specific cluster (or clusters, these can shift from moment-to-moment) being experienced. When accessed, such as then they are active in a social situation, clusters are able to be worked with and reprogrammed, just as aspects of the Narrative-Self can be in non-Finders.

Although they are subjectively experienced as separate and distinct within the psyche, clusters don't seem to be entirely independent of each other. Changing an aspect of one can ripple similar effects across others. This suggests that clusters may be constructed from underlying patterns and components that are shared among them.

Finders feel that everyone has and experiences these clusters, but that non-Finders do not realize it. They believe that the Narrative-Self "smoothes out" the experience of switching between these various, separate, and quite different "self-like" clusters. As an example, they point to the very different feeling of self and behavior that people experience at work versus home. Or, in new and uncomfortable social situations versus intimate gatherings with old friends. Yet, these differences are all smoothed over, and each of these very different selves feels like 'you.'

Some Finders believe that these clusters are "mini selves" that form the building blocks of the overall Narrative-Self. Many have mentioned that the generation of, and buying into, one's life narrative or story of self is integral to the smoothing-out process, and hides these clusters by making the Narrative-Self seem like a unified whole.

ZOOMED-IN VS. ZOOMED-OUT

There are often conflicts between the way a Finder experiences life while zoomed-in versus zoomed-out. While zoomed-out, it's common for them to have a more fully complete experience of oneness or unity, though how this manifests varies. They also often have a sense or deep feeling that everything is okay exactly as it is. Finders may experience one or both of these while zoomed-in, as well, especially if they are in a nondual location such as Location 2 or 4. However, the degree and quality of it differs.

As you can imagine, when zoomed-in the sense of fundamental okayness can be difficult to rationally accept. Looking around, one can easily see examples of poverty, violence, suffering, and so on. None of these seem morally acceptable, much less okay, to the average person. Perhaps even more interesting is that some Finders view the zoomed-in version of themselves as selfish.

There seems to be no consistent way that Finders deal with these types of disparity between their zoomed-in and zoomed-out experience. It's a bit like the schism between quantum and classical physics. While they seem to be incompatible, they nonetheless both function very well in their own ways and are clearly part of an overall whole.

Some Finders just accept that all of the suffering they see when zoomed-in is part of an overall perfection and do nothing to try to change it. Others live their day-to-day lives deeply engaged in environmental or social activism. Still others believe that there is a proper choice or way to live in each moment that is in line with "what is meant to be," and may lessen the suffering in their own lives and the lives of others.

Another example of this disparity is that, when zoomed-out, the sense of being whole and complete is maxed out. When zoomed-in this can be diminished, especially for individuals on the early end of the continuum. A full range of emotions, thoughts, doubts, and so forth can sporadically arise. To varying degrees, these types of things can occur at almost any location on the continuum, but they can be quite common in Location 1 where the range of zooming in and out is often quite limited compared to later locations. These types of paradox involving Fundamental Wellbeing and much more are examined through the lived experiences of Finders in the next section.

PART 4 – THE LIVED REALITY OF FUNDAMENTAL WELLBEING

"I have one major rule: Everybody is right. More specifically, everybody — including me — has some important pieces of truth, and all of those pieces need to be honored, cherished, and included in a more gracious, spacious, and compassionate embrace."
Ken Wilber

CHAPTER 22: VALUE JUDGMENTS, POLITICS, AND SOCIETAL IMPACT

This research project is certainly not the first to uncover parts of the continuum. Over the millennia and right up to the present, philosophers have been describing and debating the experience of Fundamental Wellbeing. The history of psychology is dotted with research on it, as well. Perhaps the most well known is Dr. Abraham Maslow, who used the phrase *peak experience* to refer to, among other things, temporary forms of the experience. As I wrote in the Introduction, towards the end of his life, Maslow began to both experience and explore persistent forms of Fundamental Wellbeing, referring to them as *high-plateau experiences*.

Religions and spiritual systems were among the earliest discoverers, explorers, and caretakers of knowledge about Fundamental Wellbeing. For example, Christian interpretations that accurately describe portions of the continuum can be found in the centuries-old writings of mystics. Similar texts are found in the other Abrahamic religions.

Information about Fundamental Wellbeing from Buddhism, Hinduism, and other Eastern traditions extends even further back, and is placed much more centrally within their doctrine. In fact, when one looks across the world's religious and spiritual traditions, it becomes obvious that many sections of the continuum have been known and explored for thousands of years. This is especially true for Locations 1, 2, and 3.

Each of these traditions makes their own value judgments about various continuum locations, including suggesting that some are more desirable than others. It's a bit like each has uncovered their own 'Goldilocks zone.' Some locations are viewed as 'too hot,' others 'too cold,' but then there are the ones that are 'just right.' This is understandable, since wellbeing does deepen as one moves further along, but in a variety of different ways.

For a faith such as Christianity, feelings of divinity increase until they reach a crescendo in the furthest reaches of Location 3. Obviously, more union with God is better within a worldview that is seeking it, so it is not surprising that they would value this location more highly than earlier or later ones.

Does this mean that Location 4 and beyond were unknown within Christianity? This seems highly unlikely. Until very recently, for Christian authors, what occurred in the transition to Location 4 was probably difficult to share without dire personal consequences and possible retributions from church hierarchy. After all, the transition from Location 3 to Location 4 takes a Christian mystic from maximum union with the divine, to the disappearance of it. For many centuries in the Christian West, professing the absence of God was not a good survival strategy.

Recently, some Christian Finders have started to discuss it. For decades, the noted Catholic mystic Bernadette Roberts (1931-2017) documented some of this later territory because she found it largely lacking in the Christian mystical literature. Her writings catalogue a personal struggle to make Location 4 and, beyond it, the Path of Freedom fit within her Catholic ideology. No doubt others before her had similar, deeply personal and private struggles but felt they couldn't be publicly shared. Some scholars feel that a few authors over the centuries did manage to write about it, in ways that obscured their true meaning.

Hints of and direct references to Location 4 and beyond are also found in other religious and spiritual traditions, especially ones that were less likely to put adherents to death for sharing their experiences. There's strong evidence that some Hindu and Buddhist sects have been aware of Location 4 for hundreds of years, possibly longer. A few even seem to have maps that extend far beyond Location 4, but these are typically kept hidden. Such groups often claim to be good at sizing up prospective adherents to determine their aptitude, and then teaching them accordingly. Only a tiny number make it to instruction about the furthest locations, and thus learn of them.

Which begs the question: if these traditions are even partially aware of Location 4 and realize the improvement in personal wellbeing it can bring, why isn't Location 4 a higher-priority goal? Perhaps this was a result of deliberate decisions that were made within these groups. For example, they may have discovered that Finders in the later stages weren't optimal for social integration. Maybe the memory issues many of these individuals experience worried them, or negatively impacted on day-to-day life within the community. It's also possible that the loss of experiencing the divine was viewed as problematic or even sacrilegious. We can only speculate at this point since there do not seem to be records detailing these decisions.

There are a handful of sects that directly focus on Location 4, and even 5+. Often these are monastic or communal. They accommodate isolated living while adherents pursue these later locations. Once Location 4 (or beyond) is reached, these Finders are typically left alone to deepen and explore their new location. Sometimes this lasts for the rest of their lives; other times familial, teaching, or mentoring obligations make them partially accessible. Sometimes partial means once every two, five, ten, or more years.

Within these groups there seems to be a general view that isolation and singular dedication is beneficial to cultivating a transition into Location 4, and beyond. Despite this, outside of these environments there are many Finders who have reached Location 4 while raising a family, holding down a job, and otherwise living a 'normal' life. However, it does seem that even these individuals reach it more rapidly with intense and dedicated focus.

SOCIETAL BENEFITS

Fundamental Wellbeing brings a lot of benefits at the individual level, but what about for society? Our data suggests that Fundamental Wellbeing has started spreading much more widely, and rapidly, since around 1995 and the dawn of the digital age. The most likely culprit in this expansion is the internet, which reached a critical mass around that time and has continued to grow ever since. It's also become clear that the pace of technological advances will help make reliable access to Fundamental Wellbeing more widely available.

Many who advocate for the widespread growth of it expect Fundamental Wellbeing to radically change human culture for the better. Some believe it will put an end to "out-of-control consumerism." Others are certain it will result in world peace, global environmentalism, or bring about similar utopian ideals. Our research doesn't point to a clear link between Fundamental Wellbeing and these types of social change.

There will undoubtedly be an impact on some forms of consumerism. A certain amount of consumer purchases are driven by the Narrative-Self trying to fill the hole at its center, and find contentment. Since Finders don't buy things to add on to who they are, some consumption will decline. However, Finders can certainly enjoy remodeling their home and playing with the latest gadget, so the net change may not be as much as the utopians hope for.

Could the growth of Fundamental Wellbeing bring about world peace? Possibly, but our data suggests that it could also increase conflict. The key seems to be how individuals become Finders. If their transition occurs within a highly dogmatic religion that advocates hostile views of others with different beliefs, new Finders can become convinced that tradition alone is God's chosen path. The absolute certainty associated with this can reduce tolerance for those with a different view, and potentially increase conflict. On the other hand, if a person shifts within a less dogmatic context the opposite can result.

The case for increased environmentalism is not any clearer. Finders typically feel deeply connected with the world. In some cases, they even experience themselves as fully at one with it. So, the thinking goes, it must naturally lead to caring more about the environment now that they identify so strongly with it.

One problem with this idea is that Finders can experience a deeper truth or sense of reality that makes the physical world seem less important. This certainly doesn't make caring for it a high priority. A second issue with this idea is much easier for anyone to understand.

To some degree, everyone associates with their body. Has this led to a world of super fit people, all of whom are obsessed with nurturing or caring for their body above all else? Hardly. So if these same people suddenly saw themselves as more than just their body, why should that lead to the assumption that they will take any better care of these extended parts of themselves?

What about morality and core values? Does becoming a Finder ensure that you cannot lie, cheat, steal, or even kill? It doesn't. There were a number of occasions during the research where blatant lies were offered up during interviews. Some of the follow-up interviews were done because parts of the initial one just didn't seem like they could be accurate. They weren't.

A tiny number of participants were also accused of participating in criminal activity after the project had interviewed them. This involved allegedly stealing, cheating people in business dealings, and similar activities. Others openly discussed it during interviews when asked. Usually the transition to Fundamental Wellbeing does not immediately, significantly affect a person's morality or values, although in some cases it does. Changes do occur over time, but they seem to go in all directions. For some, as the Narrative-Self fades along with its cultural programming, what they consider permissible widens considerably. In many instances, this increasingly puts a Finder's moral, ethical, and value systems at odds with their wider society.

No one in the study confessed to murdering someone. Some had been in wars while they experienced Fundamental Wellbeing, and had taken enemy lives. If this surprises you, it shouldn't. Over the centuries, noted warriors have also been some of their religious tradition's greatest mystics.

A utopian vision may not be realized if a significant portion of the population transitions to Fundamental Wellbeing. And, it might not put an end to crime, or killing. However, it still seems likely that it would have a significant positive impact on society.

Leading positive psychology researchers have noted many benefits that increased wellbeing brings to families and communities. Individuals with high wellbeing can be more charitable, creative, helpful, and self-confident. They often exhibit increased self-control and coping abilities. Other benefits may include: greater productivity, higher work quality, longer and more satisfying marriages, stronger social support, higher activity and energy levels, an increased sense of flow, a stronger immune system, lower stress levels, reduced amounts of pain, and even a longer life. It's not difficult to imagine the impacts these individual changes would have on society at large.

And, over time, Finders do often seem to change in more utopian directions. One interesting effect is that although personal consumption often drops, Finders do not necessarily spend less money. According to our data, many shift their spending to helping others, especially their friends and family. Some even have specific budgets for this each month, so they don't get into trouble by spending more than they can afford.

The vast majority also become much more tolerant and less prone to conflict. Even if they are dogmatic about their religion, that rarely extends into the rest of their life. In situations where the average person is likely to be argumentative, most Finders simply don't find it to be worth the energy. If you consider just these three data points—reduced personal consumption, increased charity, and a reduction in interpersonal conflict—it's easy to see the huge difference that might result in the world from more people becoming Finders. While it might not lead to a purely utopian vision, it may very well be among the few things that could dramatically impact humanity in positive ways that are critically needed right now.

One area where conflict can persist, ironically, is around Fundamental Wellbeing itself. Finders can be quite dogmatic about what it is and isn't. The next chapter explores the question of who the 'real' Finders actually are.

CHAPTER 23: I'M THE "REAL" FINDER, AND YOU'RE NOT

All Finders seem to have unique aspects to how they experience Fundamental Wellbeing. These variations, merged with their certainty, can lead them to assume that their personal experience of it is the only "proper," "correct," or "true" one. They often have a deep sense that what they are experiencing is the "Truth" (with a capital 'T') and other experiences are false, or at least less true. This can make it difficult for Finders to consider views that run contrary to their personal experience. When they interact with Finders who have another type of Fundamental Wellbeing experience, they are likely to consider them as "not quite there" or harbor doubts as to if they are even on the continuum. As time passes, this certainty can increase and lead to a form of dogmatism. This is especially true among those who have only experienced one location on the continuum.

It is easy to spot the effects of this in the marketplace of religious and spiritual ideas. Leaders and teachers often tout the superiority, or even exclusive perfection, of their form of Fundamental Wellbeing. Even within the same tradition, accomplished Finders can be found sniping at each other's authenticity.

This showed up early in the research, when Finders would be asked to contrast their experience with data from others in the study. When the information differed, it was common for Finders to suggest that the project was having difficulty understanding what was, and was not, a valid example of Fundamental Wellbeing.

Those with an in-depth knowledge of at least one religious or spiritual system often backed up their view with stories and dogma from their tradition. For example, when one well-known Buddhist teacher was asked about a person who was in Location 4, the teacher argued that the person was 'stuck' in a certain Jhana (a highly specific state of, usually temporary, consciousness) and was not experiencing Fundamental Wellbeing. At the time, this teacher was a well-known 'Jhana Master' who was able to enter these various states at will. His certainty was so strong that he actually entered into the Jhana he was referring to so he could be interviewed in that state for comparison.

Not long afterwards, this teacher learned that one of his former students (also a participant in the research) had shifted into Location 4. The reports from this student caused the teacher to reconsider his position. He decided to accept the possibility that a persistent state of consciousness involving no emotion or agency could also be considered a valid form of Fundamental Wellbeing, and explore it. The last time I saw him, he was advocating for Fluid 4 being the most desirable experience of the continuum, though it is certainly possible that he has changed his views again since.

Because some forms of Fundamental Wellbeing bring such a deep sense of truth and certainty, it is understandable that Finders imagine their experience of it is the "correct" version. This often only changes when they walk a mile in another location's shoes, by shifting to a new place on the continuum. Such a transition can bring as much, or more, "certainty" and "Truth" as the previous location, but with a different perspective. This can force a softening of their view, and even cause Finders to accept that other shifts may be possible. This change in perspective can allow them to be more accepting of their own experiences and what others describe to them.

Ironically, it also seems to make them more likely to have their experiences discredited by those who have not shifted locations. Remaining in a single continuum location can harden a Finder's sense of certainty. Its relatively unchanging nature is viewed as further evidence that the experience is the truest form of Fundamental Wellbeing. As a result, these individuals often view others who have experienced more than one location on the continuum as not actually being "true Finders."

FLAVORS OF TRUTH

Finders who have moved back and forth between locations often observe that each location brings a distinct flavor of "Truth." Something that seems true to a Finder in Location 3 might not seem true at all in Location 4. Instead, a very different "Truth" might emerge to take its place. However, if the person later shifts back to Location 3, these will flip. What seemed true at Location 4 will seem less true, or even totally false. What originally seemed true the first time they were in Location 3 will seem true again.

Finders who move on the continuum are generally able to contextualize the "Truth" of a given location. With each shift, the Truth that comes into focus becomes more nuanced. It's common for them to say that their first transition from a 'lower' to 'higher' location felt like it was accompanied by an increased depth and degree of Truth. However, subsequent shifts lead to interpreting these differences less simplistically. These Finders report that there is a very specific feeling of Truth that accompanies, and is appropriate, to each location they shift into.

RELIGIOUS AND SPIRITUAL TRUTH

Previously we touched upon the idea that the life experiences Finders arrive with when they land on the continuum can have an impact on the feeling of Truth that comes with it. Those who experience their shift in association with a religion are more likely to adopt that religion's doctrine as true. This is the case even if they previously had an "all paths to God are okay"-type attitude. Their new belief can be so strong that these Finders can even find themselves arguing against the dogma of other sects within their religion.

If an atheist or agnostic happens to shift into Fundamental Wellbeing while in a religious or spiritual context, s/he can become a powerful and dogmatic convert. Though rare, this can even happen if the transition occurs during a casual conversation with a religious leader or spiritual teacher. Conversely, if the transition to Fundamental Wellbeing occurs outside of a religious context, even if someone is highly religious, it is less likely to be strongly associated with and guided by religious belief. If the Finder was highly devout before Fundamental Wellbeing, s/he may still be afterwards. However, if the shift didn't occur within a religious context or setting, his or her dogmatism may weaken. This is even more the case for less religious individuals who shift into Fundamental Wellbeing. Many of these Finders leave religion altogether.

All of this hints at what some Finders have been fortunate enough to discover first hand, that the experience of Fundamental Wellbeing is malleable and can be "tuned." Most never discover this, because they don't think to experiment around and see if it is the case. A handful, however, have no choice and their circumstances are examined in the next chapter.

CHAPTER 24: YOU GET WHAT YOU OPTIMIZE FOR

We've already seen that numerous factors can influence how Fundamental Wellbeing manifests differently in people. Most typically, Finders happen into a specific type of Fundamental Wellbeing and remain locked in it from that point forward. But, this doesn't have to be the case. Many things including the Finder's ideology, cultural imprints, biology, and so forth, can combine to influence the way it unfolds.

While some of these appear to be 'hardwired' into Finders and out of their control, other elements can be consciously manipulated to shape the experience in preferred ways. For example, Christian mystics tend to focus on the experience of the divine, while Buddhists often have a different emphasis such as spaciousness or emptiness.

Beneath these lie the deeper structures that relate to each location on the continuum. This is another aspect of Fundamental Wellbeing that can be consciously shaped. A Finder in Location 2 who learns about Location 3 can pursue it, and usually get there. For some, their shift to the new location will be rapid, and for others it may take years or decades.

We are just beginning to understand how flexible the experience of Fundamental Wellbeing can be. The potential combinations of these surface and deeper aspects are potentially limitless. At present, there certainly does not seem to be a 'correct' version.

A key limitation comes from the structure of language itself. The words and phrases we use were created by and in support of the way the Narrative-Self views the world. This makes Fundamental Wellbeing difficult to convey to those who do not share the same experiences. Similarly, Finders can be trapped in the words and descriptions of their religious or spiritual traditions. These lead to beliefs that directly control not only how Fundamental Wellbeing unfolds, but how far they are likely to progress on the continuum.

At a specific continuum location, the experience of Fundamental Wellbeing within a tradition is often similar, but the experience for each person is unique. The generalized, standardized, community-agreed-upon descriptions can blur the variances between Finders. However, when asked to describe the details of their first-person experience, differences between them emerge. Even individuals who have studied and practiced their religion or spiritual system together, in the same place, for decades can arrive at different versions of Fundamental Wellbeing.

Sometimes, these variations can be more in sync with individuals outside of their tradition than those within it. Think of it this way: there might be only a handful of people within a given tradition who experience Location 4. However, there are many others from different traditions, or no tradition, at this location. How these very diverse individuals experience Location 4 in terms of cognition, emotion, perception, and memory will be similar regardless of a Finder's background. But the surface-level flavor, which often includes the specific aspects of the location that are emphasized and valued, and the way Finders use language to express their experiences of the location, may be quite different.

Because everyone within their tradition is using similar language, Finders often assume that they are all experiencing Fundamental Wellbeing in similar ways. For example, a small percentage of individuals who participate in the Christian conversion ritual of 'asking Jesus to enter your heart' transition to Fundamental Wellbeing as a result. These newly minted Finders generally assume that this happens for everyone.

Christian mysticism, and its knowledge of different continuum locations, does not penetrate very deeply into mainstream churches. Despite this, many of the prayers, songs, and other standardized terminology in the religion reflect a vague and generalized experience of Fundamental Wellbeing. These shape the language used by believers. It can make it seem like everyone is experiencing Fundamental Wellbeing, and that there is a standard experience of it. Christian Finders who got there through this conversion experience are often shocked to discover that neither is the case.

My own mother is one of them. When I began this line of research, she considered it preposterous because she assumed that anyone who had asked Jesus to come into their heart experienced Fundamental Wellbeing. What good could possibly come from studying something that was so easily attained and ubiquitous? Her mother and father were both Finders, roughly in Locations 2 and 3 respectively. And she had been on the continuum since the day she accepted Christ as a young child.

She assumed I had experienced it since asking Jesus to come into my heart at age 4 while we lived in Hong Kong, and was shocked that it wasn't the case. After a bit of soul searching, she had to admit that she wasn't at all sure that her brothers and sisters experienced it. And, although she'd never thought about it, the transition for her father didn't happen right away, but instead decades after his conversion. The fact that everyone singing hymns next to her in church each week wasn't a Finder was a genuine paradigm shift. They sure sounded like it while singing, praying, and discussing the Bible from a perspective of Fundamental Wellbeing alongside her!

SHAPING THE EXPERIENCE OF FUNDAMENTAL WELLBEING

Unlike those with religious, spiritual, or philosophical knowledge about Fundamental Wellbeing, some individuals have no frame of reference for it before their transition. This can make the early flavor of their experience highly flexible and fluid. They often begin to understand Fundamental Wellbeing in one of three ways. Some find another person who is familiar with at least one form of it. Others wander into a library or bookstore, and eventually stumble across materials that seem related to it. Still others search the internet and essentially do the same online.

Before the internet, the bookstore or library scenario was the most common. These Finders would eventually find books on spirituality or the mystical aspects of a specific religion in which they could somewhat make out their experience. More recently, the internet changed everything. Now, a new Finder can easily find both relevant information and other Finders online.

The fascinating thing about these Finders is that as they do their research their initial experience of Fundamental Wellbeing is changed and colored by the descriptions of it they encounter. Some read more and find that doing so deepens and locks in that flavor. Others search out and find additional perspectives. When they do, their experience often shifts and morphs along with what they are reading. The savviest explore widely and, essentially, select the form of Fundamental Wellbeing they find most appealing.

This may be one reason certain traditions emphasize training in compassion, or stress the importance of love. Perhaps long ago their adherents or leaders decided it was personally or societally desirable to have a certain flavor of Fundamental Wellbeing. It's not hard to see the outcomes produced by various inputs when you look across a diverse sample of Finders. Very early in the research, the "you get what you optimize for" idea was evident.

Of course, this requires that value judgments be made. Looking at the most developed traditions, it certainly seems as though they may have been deliberately shaped by these types of decisions. Is love and compassion of core importance? Or, is going beyond all emotion to even deeper wellbeing the most desirable? Or, something else entirely?

It is likely that our society will face a point when we will be making similar value judgments regarding how Fundamental Wellbeing is best experienced. This already appears to be happening among Finders. There are significant debates in the public, as well as in academic circles about the importance of it including emotions like love, or virtues such as specific forms of compassion. As Fundamental Wellbeing becomes increasingly common, subcultures within our society will adopt their own norms and standardized viewpoints. Over time, individuals will be influenced by this process and do the same.

Perhaps some will favor experiences of a loving divinity, while others standardize on the feeling of an all-pervasive consciousness. Or, there may be a preference for experiencing the emotional deliciousness of Location 3, over the positively-biased emotional flexibility of Location 2. Perhaps all of that will be shunned for Location 4. Hopefully the data presented here, and related research efforts, will be allowed to shine some light on these choices so that conflicts and arguments over which flavor is the 'correct one' can be minimized.

Degree of persistence also enters into this debate. It's not uncommon for people to have a temporary, or so-called 'peak' experience that shifts their worldview profoundly, and mistake this change for Fundamental Wellbeing. On the other hand, some people miss the Fundamental Wellbeing that can sometimes settle in after the intensity of a peak experience dies down. Many transition to Fundamental Wellbeing without ever having a peak experience. The next chapter tackles all of this, and more.

CHAPTER 25: TEMPORARY OR PERSISTENT?

Many individuals experience Fundamental Wellbeing for only a few moments. For others, the experience might last for days, weeks, or even months. To be a Finder, your Fundamental Wellbeing has to be persistent and ongoing. Our data suggests that if it has lasted for over seven months, it will probably stick around for the long haul.

Temporary forms of Fundamental Wellbeing are reported in a wide range of circumstances. Sometimes they are triggered when someone is looking out at a beautiful scene. Others have experienced them while taking a psychedelic drug. Illness has been shown to produce them, as have near death experiences. Ritual, dancing, meditation, and intense physical exercise all seem to have the possibility of bringing them on. These are just a small sample from the much longer lists generated by researchers who inquire into these phenomena.

As mentioned previously, perhaps the greatest overall study on temporary forms of Fundamental Wellbeing was conducted by the famous psychologist Dr. Abraham Maslow. He referred to Fundamental Wellbeing as peak experiences. Although his descriptions of them run into many pages, the shorthand is that they are a psychological state that takes one beyond the Narrative-Self. They can include intense emotions, as well as feelings of ecstasy, euphoria, unity, harmony, and interconnectedness. They can also have a noetic quality where deeper 'Truth' is revealed, as well as a spiritual or religious character.

These temporary experiences often depart as mysteriously as they arrive, however they can leave deep and lasting psychological transformation in their wake. They typically involve a state of high physiological arousal. The ecstatic and euphoric descriptors referred to previously are examples of this. This is a significant difference between temporary and persistent forms of Fundamental Wellbeing.

Sometimes a Finder will experience higher levels of physiological arousal in the moments or weeks following their transition to Fundamental Wellbeing, but it rarely lasts. In fact, the opposite is usually experienced. It brings about a deep inner peace that can cause some Finders to wish for more energy. Maslow noticed this as well, noting in the 1970 preface to his classic book *Religions, Values, and Peak Experiences* that persistent Fundamental Wellbeing involved: more serenity and calm, a blissful cognitive element, and a degree of relaxation that is not typically the case for temporary forms of the experience.

The transition into Fundamental Wellbeing is obvious for most people. However, there is one version of the experience that can make it difficult to determine if you are experiencing a temporary or persistent form. On the early end of the continuum, Finders can be embedded in an environment that is triggering their conditioning and pushing down their inner peace. These individuals can assume that they are frequently going in and out of temporary episodes of Fundamental Wellbeing, rather than experiencing a persistent form of it.

A good way to determine if it is persistent is to ask whether some form of it, however faint, always seems to be present. Another way to tackle this question is to compare these moments to Maslow's descriptions of peak experiences, and then to the description of Fundamental Wellbeing contained in this book. For example, does high physiological arousal accompany them? In most instances, these two tests should help make this potentially confusing situation clear.

As we'll see in the next chapter, persistence can mean different things to different Finders. For some, it means experiencing Fundamental Wellbeing while awake, but then losing awareness during sleep. Surprisingly, for others persistence is a 24/7 affair.

CHAPTER 26: 24/7 PERSISTENCE

Fundamental Wellbeing can feel like gaining access to a very deep and foundational level of awareness. This helps to explain some of the spiritual terms for it, like the *ground of all being*. In this book, the phrase 'Fundamental Wellbeing' generally refers to the persistent experience of it while awake. However, there are some traditions that believe this should extend further, into sleep.

Everyone can be awoken from deep sleep, so some degree of awareness must be present and monitoring what's happening. A minority of Finders can access this level of awareness, and report on it. They essentially remain aware 24 hours a day, seven days a week (24/7). There doesn't seem to be any relationship between a Finder's degree of 24/7 awareness and their location on the continuum.

Some traditions explicitly link 24/7 awareness with one or more locations, usually later ones. However, simply having this expectation doesn't seem to make it more likely to happen. Reports of it weren't any more prevalent among individuals who experience Fundamental Wellbeing from those traditions, than from Finders in general.

Many of the research participants had never experienced 24/7 awareness. Of those who did, most only experienced it for limited periods of time. For some, it only happened once. For others, it had come and gone over their time as a Finder. Only a tiny percentage of participants claimed to have 24/7 awareness as part of their long-term, ongoing experience. A handful even reported being able to turn it on and off.

The 24/7 experience makes ongoing awareness a constant companion, and yields an even deeper sense of certainty and truth than other continuum-based experiences. Some research participants had lived with this 24/7 awareness for so many years that it had simply become 'normal.' Even for these Finders, there was one thing that seemed to reliably be able to impact it.

Undergoing surgery removed the sense of awareness while they were under anesthesia. Over time, they had come to assume their experience of awareness was rock solid and could not be affected by anything. That it was foundational. Its temporary outage while they were under the knife often shook their most deeply held beliefs.

What does awareness in sleep feel like? There isn't a uniform answer. Some seem able to observe their bodies go to sleep, watch the various stages of it, and view the waking up process. For others, only some portions of sleep seem to have this degree of specificity. Still others just have a vague sense of being aware, but nothing that can be described in detail.

No discussion of sleep is complete without mentioning dreams. Not all Finders report dreams. Among those who do, only some experience them consistently. Some dream in color, others only in black and white, and still others both. For those with greater awareness in sleep, dreams are often witnessed in a detached way. Others are drawn more deeply into dreams, which may or may not be lucid. Lucid dreams are those in which the dreamer has conscious awareness that s/he is dreaming, and can sometimes exercise a degree of control. Some Finders take this a step further, and report being able to rewind and replay their dreams. There are also Finders who believe that dreamtime can be important for deepening and progressing in Fundamental Wellbeing. Views on this range from it being a good place to process and work on conditioning, to how the Buddhist tradition views "dream Yoga."

Finally, the amount of sleep is another thing that can vary with Fundamental Wellbeing. Some Finders report a reduced need for sleep. This varies a great deal, with a minority saying that they only sleep for a few hours a week, if that. Others report needing only one to four hours a night. Most sleep the 'normal' six to eight hours. It's relatively common for Finders to discuss going through periods where they sleep much more or less than normal per day. Periods where sleep exceeded 10 hours were commonly reported, as were periods where sleep was minimal or even nonexistent.

The average person couldn't imagine going for long periods without traditional sleep. Among other things, sleep is instrumental in cleansing

144

our brain of toxins each night. It's difficult to understand why this doesn't lead to cognitive impairment or even illness in Finders. It shows how, in many ways, research into Fundamental Wellbeing is still in its infancy.

The next chapter examines a topic no Finder wants to consider, and many don't even believe is possible: losing Fundamental Wellbeing and returning to 'normal.' Although it wasn't a focus of the study, many former Finders contacted the research project over the years who were looking to get it back. Fundamental Wellbeing is definitely not something that should be considered permanent. We use the term persistent to highlight that fact. It should be respected and cultivated if you want it to last for the rest of your life, regardless of how long you've experienced it. It's very useful to know what makes it go away if you want it to stick around.

CHAPTER 27: THE LOSS OF FUNDAMENTAL WELLBEING

Over the years, the publicity surrounding this research project has attracted people who claimed to be former Finders. Usually these individuals contacted the project hoping to learn how they could re-enter Fundamental Wellbeing. They had generally lived in it for many years before it went away. One person experienced it for twenty-three years before illness pushed him out of it.

Many Finders believe that Fundamental Wellbeing cannot be lost, and that "real" Finders will never lose their experience of it. Virtually all believe that it is present in everyone, but simply unrecognized. They might comment, for example, that although "normal" experience can obscure it, Fundamental Wellbeing is always present as the foundation of all awareness.

Those whose personal experience of Fundamental Wellbeing has not changed significantly over time are most likely to believe that it is permanent and unshakable. When asked about those who seem to have lost it, these Finders often state that the individuals probably never fully experienced it. Most of those who lost it admitted to similar beliefs when they experienced it. Finders that personally know someone who lost their experience of Fundamental Wellbeing are more likely to accept that it could happen to them.

So, what makes it go away? Some former Finders reported its loss due to brain injury or other illness. Most reported losing it during an extremely stressful time in their lives. A few did not have any specific event or occurrence that seemed to explain it. Because the research focused on persistence, full interviews weren't conducted with most of these former Finders. Anecdotally, it appeared that Locations 1 through 4 were all involved.

Returning to the psychological suffering that the average person experiences can be traumatic for a Finder. Perhaps most surprising, when Fundamental Wellbeing vanishes, these individuals essentially land back in their former sense of self. Not only do they return to a Narrative-Self, but to the one they left behind. It's almost like it was in hibernation waiting for them to return.

There were some changes, of course. Often these relate to the conditioning that was eliminated during the transition to Fundamental Wellbeing or while the person experienced it. Some of this simply didn't come back. Those who were extremely depressed when they transitioned, for example, were less depressed. But, they generally weren't happy. They knew what they were missing and were desperately trying to get it back.

Some former Finders discussed how happy they considered themselves prior to Fundamental Wellbeing. These individuals were stunned to experience the additional levels of wellbeing that were possible within it. Even though they often returned to a "happy" Narrative-Self, the contrast between it and Fundamental Wellbeing was pronounced.

The implications here are remarkable. Religious and spiritual traditions often refer to the transformation that occurs with Fundamental Wellbeing. It's not uncommon for them to believe that the "old self" was "burned away," "purified," "consumed," "born again," or some similar notion; but this does not seem to be the case. While we can't be certain of the degree to which this may happen, the experiences of these former Finders certainly seem to suggest that, at a minimum, it isn't always the case. While they were experiencing a new sense of self, their former one stuck around in a way that was later able to be reactivated.

This is not surprising from a neuroscience viewpoint. Unless there is damage from illness or injury, the default view in modern neuroscience is that most connections in the brain are quite persistent. When they are not used, they atrophy, but most never fully go away. They are waiting to be brought back to life. The degree to which this is likely often depends on a variety of factors, from how long they have been mostly or fully unused, to the strength of the psychological experience that deactivated them in the first place.

Although many people think that changes in the brain happen slowly over time, the reality is that many happen quite rapidly. Scientists who operate high-quality imaging systems know that brains can change significantly over measurements that are just a few minutes apart.

Post-traumatic stress disorder (PTSD) is an example of massive change in the brain happening in a very short period of time. In these instances, a significant and traumatic life event happens and the brain rewires right away and very persistently in a way that often has a significantly negative impact on a person's life. Some existing connections in the brain fall immediately dormant, while new ones appear that produce the negative impact.

Peak experiences, positive near-death experiences, and positive psychedelic experiences are examples of the opposite of PTSD. These types of events can rapidly deactivate negative connections and form or emphasize existing positive ones. These can remain active for a very long time. There are many examples in the scientific research literature of these types of life events creating persistent, positive change in people's lives.

Many people who pursue Fundamental Wellbeing believe in doing psychological and other self-help work as part of the process. The idea is to clean up their psychological baggage as much as possible before they transition. There are even those that suggest you should put off transitioning to Fundamental Wellbeing until you have reached a certain level of "internal cleanliness."

To date, the research project has not detected any clear-cut patterns in terms of what does and does not get deactivated during the transition to Fundamental Wellbeing, or between locations. Our advice up to this point has been to transition, see what psychological baggage remains, and then go from there. Otherwise, for example, you might spend years trying to clear up a childhood trauma, believing that it was essential to do so before your transition to Fundamental Wellbeing, when in fact it would have become irrelevant because of changes that occurred during your transition.

One of the most interesting things about Fundamental Wellbeing is that stress is the number one cause of losing it. On the surface, this seems very counter-intuitive. In the next chapter, we explore why people who feel such a deep sense of internal peace can get pulled out of Fundamental Wellbeing entirely by, often unfelt, stress.

CHAPTER 28: STRESS AND FUNDAMENTAL WELLBEING

It was a huge surprise that so many of the former Finders believed extreme stress was the reason they lost their Fundamental Wellbeing. After all, the scores on stress measures given to research participants were very low.

The first hint of this was a woman who approached us at a speaking engagement. After five years of Fundamental Wellbeing, she lost it during a phase when her life fell apart. Over a short period of time, her father died, her son was ill and possibly dying, and her husband of many years left her. When asked about her internal state during this period, she said that it was her usual sense of Fundamental Wellbeing. Initially, we just filed the report away and apologized for not having an answer for how she could get back. It seemed too improbable that unfelt and undetected stress could lead to a loss of Fundamental Wellbeing.

As time went on and our database grew, more individuals made the same claim. It became clear that a deeper look was warranted. An effort was made to collect additional details about the current life circumstances of participants, in part to look for stressful situations. This yielded three research opportunities where it seemed like a participant's stress level might be high enough to warrant a follow-up visit.

As luck would have it, our very first interviewee, my doctor friend, was one of them. As mentioned previously, I had known him for over twenty years, since long before he had become a Finder. During his initial interview, he was in Location 2. By the time of the stress research, he had not changed locations, though he later transitioned to Location 3.

Over the course of a very short period of time, his father and sister both died. He was also going through a significant issue with one of his adult children. Over dinner, when asked about his internal state, he

151

reported it as deeply peaceful and positive despite everything that was happening.

Eventually, his girlfriend and a fellow researcher who was present left the table and went to the bar. While getting drinks, his significant other was asked about any signs of stress the participant might be exhibiting. I casually asked the same questions to my friend as we continued our dinner conversation.

The answers couldn't have been more different. While he reported no stress, his partner had been observing many telltale signs: he wasn't sleeping well, his appetite was off, his mood was noticeably different, his muscles were more tense than normal, his sex drive was reduced, his overall health seemed to be suffering, and so forth. The same dichotomy was observed in the other two participants who were in high stress situations.

As data collection continued around this phenomenon, a series of experiments were set up to try to learn more. It seemed as if there might be a significant disconnect between Finders' internal subjective experience and what their physical body revealed. This was especially pronounced during times of high stress, but eventually it became clear that it was broadly measurable as well.

It's common for Finders to say that they feel more in tune with their body and its sensations since transitioning into Fundamental Wellbeing. This makes sense if you consider their reports of increased present-moment and heightened sensory awareness. In one of the earliest experiments, we explored the bodily awareness of this research participant through a private yoga session. The session was facilitated by a doctoral candidate and long-time researcher on the project, who is also a highly experienced international yoga instructor.

During the session, it became clear that the participant believed he was far more aware of his body than was actually the case. For example, the researcher would put her hand on part of the participant's body while he was in a yoga position, and ask him to relax the tense muscles there. The Finder usually insisted that he was totally relaxed in that area, and did not feel any muscle tension. The amount of tension in the musculature was visible both to the naked eye and on the camera recordings that were made to document the research.

Over the years, further exploration of this phenomenon revealed a similar pattern. It is common for participants to feel more connected and in-tune with their bodies than is actually the case. This often continues to grow the further along the continuum someone goes.

THE BENEFITS OF STRESS FOR FINDERS

Stress is a fact of life. In some cases, it will cause a Finder to shift back to an earlier location on the continuum. In extreme cases, it causes some to fall completely out of Fundamental Wellbeing. But, stress can be a double-edged sword.

Some of the most dramatic transitions reported during the research were from high stress situations that propelled Finders further along the continuum. Individuals seemed to jump past or rapidly advance through one or more locations to reach a later one. This was especially true for stress associated with cathartic moments that revolved around intense psychological conditioning from earlier in their life.

For example, a Finder who had a very difficult family life while growing up might later have to care for the family members that once made his or her life a nightmare. The stress and friction involved in this can lead to intense psychological drama, and thus deconditioning. Plus, an entirely new level of psychological release can occur when one or more of the family members dies. In cases such as this, it is common for new locations to be reached as major milestones occur in the Finder's own psychological healing process. It seems that even Finders routinely underestimate how the patterns laid down in early childhood and young adulthood can have profoundly limiting effects later in life, and in this case, how far they can travel along the continuum.

The stress doesn't have to be family related. It's just as possible for intense stress at work or in other areas of a Finder's life to cause a similar shift to occur. Some Finders who had transitioned to and remained in a single location for decades reported that the stress of an event was what shook them into one or more other locations.

Given the dual nature of stress and its impact on Finders, it does not seem like a safe path to explore for deepening. It might take a Finder further, or it might pull them out of Fundamental Wellbeing entirely.

Losing Fundamental Wellbeing is one thing, rejecting it is quite another. Although it's rare, some people chose not to live as a Finder. Actually, choice may not be the right word, as you'll see in the next chapter.

CHAPTER 29: REJECTING FUNDAMENTAL WELLBEING

Once the research started, it immediately became clear that almost no one wanted to get rid of their Fundamental Wellbeing. Finders highly preferred it to their previous way of experiencing the world. However, over time, individuals did emerge who had rejected it. Some people simply did not prefer it, regardless of what location they landed in. A major reason for this was because the change they experienced in motivation after their transition to Fundamental Wellbeing produced negative impacts on their income, social life, or other aspects of their life, and they simply decided to switch back.

Many people who rejected Fundamental Wellbeing had one major thing in common: they had experienced rapid transitions that took them directly into Location 4. In one case, a person read a book about Fundamental Wellbeing, went to sleep, and woke up in Location 4. Despite being absorbed in a previously undreamt-of level of wellbeing and sense of freedom, he felt he'd traded his humanity for it. It is not uncommon for those who land in Location 4 without religious or spiritual moorings or a psychological frame of reference to feel this way. The lack of agency and emotion feels so different than what they had recognized as normal up to that point. The turning point for this person was looking across the breakfast table at his young daughter, and not feeling even the slightest tinge of parental love.

Reports like this may seem at odds with the absence of agency. It certainly sounds like someone is debating things and making a decision. And, it seems, a debate is going on internally. The difference is that, to a Location 4 Finder, it feels like the debate is "just happening." It does not feel as if the person, as an individual, is wrapped up in it. However, it is clear that the brain seems to be mulling the situation over. Thinking and analysis still happen; it just doesn't feel like there is any sense of a

Narrative-Self that is weighing things in a self-referential way for what is best. Even this changes after a period of time; a deepening occurs in Location 4 that eliminates these types of debates. You'll learn more about that soon.

To date, the rejecters we've spoken to have reported that it took them between 2 weeks and 8 months to return to their previous sense of self. It took this person three months. He didn't appear to regret his decision at all.

REJECTING LOCATION 4

Occasionally, Finders will report rejecting the shift to a new location on the continuum. This almost always involves moving into Location 4, since it often conflicts with deeply held beliefs and ideologies. Though, again, it's important to note that there usually isn't a sense of agency involved. To the Finder, it appears as if the debate and subsequent rejection just happen.

At Location 3, religious Finders usually experience an intense union with the divine. This creates a deep certainty within them involving their faith, and is generally validated by their tradition as correct. Its sudden absence can be jarring and convince them that something has gone wrong, even though their wellbeing and sense of freedom have increased. This observation is often solidified by consultations with their most trusted references and spiritual advisors.

One research participant's principal spiritual teacher did not understand the Location 4 experience. Although the teacher was highly respected and experienced, her beliefs placed significant emphasis on positive emotion, especially love. When the Finder sought advice, the teacher advised rejecting Location 4. To this teacher, it seemed like something had gone terribly wrong in her student's consciousness.

The sense of perfection experienced in Location 4 convinced the process happening within this Finder that it did not matter where someone was in life, or consciousness. It seemed like everything truly was and could only be perfect and that this would be true regardless of whether she remained in Location 4, or returned to an earlier location.

The participant was in her late twenties, but had already been on the continuum for many years. The process unfolding in her seemed to recognize that there were many aspects of the human condition that could be experienced from earlier locations, but not Location 4. For example, she had not yet found her romantic partner, nor had she experienced the intensity of parental love.

At the same time, this impersonal process seemed to be observing how it felt to live in Location 4. It sensed the isolation that was produced involving her friends, and humanity as a whole. Inside, the experience of living was so utterly different from everyone around her.

On the other hand, the sense of freedom pouring through her was far beyond anything she could have imagined. For the first time, there was absolute liberation from needing any approval from others. Ultimately, the process unfolding inside her seemed to reach a conclusion that Location 4 could be transitioned to again at a later time. Within two weeks the participant was back to an earlier location on the continuum.

This degree of depth and complexity sheds important light on concepts such as 'correct,' 'better,' or 'more developed' forms of Fundamental Wellbeing. It allows us to glimpse inside the experience of a Finder who has experienced Locations 1 through 4 on the continuum. Despite the deeper wellbeing and greater sense of freedom it offered, when Location 4 initially came calling, it was rejected.

The debate that was kicked off in her around it is very telling. Her consciousness took into consideration the experience itself, options of others, best guess estimates of being able to return to the location later, and more. In a sense, this looks like almost any other rational decision-making process, the key exception being that it occurred inside someone who felt that they were mostly just observing it unfold.

HOW TO REJECT LOCATION 4

All of the rejecters encountered during the research used a similar technique to exit Location 4. Even though they were no longer experiencing emotion, it appeared that deep, hidden emotional and psychological triggers remained in them. These could occasionally produce weak, "ghost-like" sensations, another form of the proto-emotions that were referred to in a previous chapter. As a Finder deepens in Location 4, these ghost-like pieces of former emotions vanish. Before this point is reached, though, they can be used to exit Location 4.

Each rejecter learned that if they put themselves in situations that produced these proto-emotions, they could focus on and strengthen them. It's a simple and logical solution. Look for something internally that seems like it might relate to how reality was previously experienced, and try to latch on to it. Eventually these sensations reformed into emotions. Focusing on and strengthening these emotions led out of Location 4. The individuals were either returned to an earlier point on the continuum, or to a narrative sense of self.

Many people regard Location 4 as a type of Fundamental Wellbeing that seems a bit far out. Discussions of it often lead to people asking about 'unusual' things they've heard about Finders and what they might be able to do—like read minds or see the future. Stories of abilities like this have been part of the selling proposition around Fundamental Wellbeing in some spiritual and religious traditions for millennia. The possibilities are explored in the next chapter.

CHAPTER 30: SPECIAL ABILITIES

Most people have a spiritual or religious tradition. For these individuals, the concept of Fundamental Wellbeing is often powerfully interwoven with the stories of their saints, masters, gurus, and mystics. Some of these individuals directly claimed, or were said to have demonstrated, "special abilities" such as being able to read minds, see the past and future, heal the sick, and so forth. As strange as they may sound, levitation, passing part or all of one's physical body through a solid object, disappearing, manifesting unusual visual phenomena (such as a glowing light), pushing a solid object through a different one, and manifesting objects from thin air are mentioned across many traditions. Because some aspects of this were covered in the chapter on Location 5+, this chapter deals only with these reports as they related to research participants in Locations 1 through 4.

When asked about during interviews, reports of these types of experiences were exceedingly rare. The Finders who did make claims involving them were spread across the continuum. By contrast, Finders quite commonly reported increases in both the frequency and accuracy of their intuition, though very few considered it related to the 'special abilities' listed at the beginning of this chapter. Believing that they'd gotten a glimpse of someone else's thoughts was the next most common report. Only a handful suggested that they had experienced any of the more esoteric examples.

Some spiritual and religious traditions believe that these types of experiences go hand-in-glove with Fundamental Wellbeing. They may even base the truth of someone's claim to being a Finder on them. This isn't surprising, because Fundamental Wellbeing is an internal experience.

How can anyone really know, from the outside, if someone else is experiencing it? But if they can levitate or manifest objects out of thin air, perhaps it proves that they really are tapped into the deeper truths of the Universe. Of course, this has opened the door to more than a few charlatans using sleight of hand and other trickery, trying to convince people they are a genuine Finder.

Other traditions warn their adherents not to get caught up in these types of abilities. They often stress that they can detract from the overall goal of Fundamental Wellbeing. Or, a tradition may have dogma around some of these abilities being good, while others are evil.

There are also traditions that say nothing about these types of things in relation to Fundamental Wellbeing. They may or may not even have views on the subject. If they do, most often these types of potential abilities are not viewed as relevant in any way to Fundamental Wellbeing.

Phenomena associated with these various 'special abilities' are reported by a wide variety of people around the world. If they exist, it is unclear if Finders experience them any more than others do. Research participants from traditions that believe in 'special abilities' were not more likely to report experiencing them. These types of abilities, capabilities, skills, delusions, or whatever you want to classify them as do not seem to be required components of Fundamental Wellbeing.

As this book goes to press, the research project is in the early stages of a new sub-project investigating these types of claims. If validated, these types of experiences would cause a seismic shift in what we consider possible as humans. We'd love to hear from or about more people who believe they have these types of abilities and are open to scientific research.

One of the most sought-after 'special abilities' is being able to directly shift someone into Fundamental Wellbeing. After all, why go through years of trial and error if you can just find the right person to tap you on the shoulder and send you directly to Location 3? Some of our research participants reported this. The next chapter covers what we learned from them.

CHAPTER 31: CAN FUNDAMENTAL WELLBEING RUB OFF ON YOU?

It's not uncommon for spiritually-oriented people to believe that Finders can transmit a temporary or persistent experience of Fundamental Wellbeing to others. Or, that just being in the vicinity of a Finder can assist with facilitating a shift in consciousness. A small number of research participants did report experiencing this emanating from them, and some believed they transitioned because of another Finder producing it in them. Of the former, some said they occasionally felt such a transmission happen "on its own." Others stated they could produce it on demand, though not all the time. Still others felt it flowing through them at all times and believed those around them could receive it as a blessing.

Non-Finders who believe in this often travel long distances to be near Finders who stress the importance of it. They might even go halfway around the world, from a country such as the United States to somewhere like Thailand or India.

Length of exposure to a Finder is also viewed as something that might be helpful. A surprising number of people make dramatic lifestyle decisions to spend more time around someone who is experiencing Fundamental Wellbeing. This may involve choosing to live for a while in a guru's ashram, cloistering away in a mystic's monastery, or simply moving to be closer to a Finder with a day job who lives in a Chicago suburb.

Family and friends are probably the best evidence against the exposure hypothesis. During our research, it was unusual for a Finder's family to experience Fundamental Wellbeing. Practically speaking, it's hard to imagine you could have more time around these individuals than their families do. The same is true for friends, co-workers, and others who have significant exposure but also almost never experience Fundamental Wellbeing.

Before the internet, the best hope for connecting directly to a Finder was often through his or her writings. A small percentage of participants reported shifting into Fundamental Wellbeing this way. The works spanned all faiths and time periods, and didn't have to be from someone's core tradition. Of course, it is possible that the ideas in these books simply triggered something in the reader's psychology. Their shift might have had nothing to do with forming some kind of connection to, or resonance with, the writer.

Today, anyone can easily connect with hundreds of Finders from around the world online. They can be emailed, found on forums and blogs, watched on YouTube, and even chatted with in real time using text, voice, video, or all three. Our data suggests that the amount of people transitioning to Fundamental Wellbeing has been increasing significantly since the mid- to late-nineties. Two obvious potential contributing factors are the growth in internet connectivity since that time, and the ever-increasing amount of information about Fundamental Wellbeing that can be found online.

IS IT IMPORTANT TO MEET A FINDER?

Some individuals do transition after meeting a Finder. Most had been actively working toward Fundamental Wellbeing for some time, but the shift didn't occur until this direct contact. Many felt that the language, phrases, and information given in-person were no different than what they found in the Finder's writings and recordings. In some cases, they were just one person in a large audience the Finder was speaking to. Yet, for some reason, the shift occurred during or after seeing the person.

These participants clearly regarded these meetings as significant. They were typically deeply grateful for the Finder who took time to interact with them. Of course, the research project engaged mostly with Finders. It's certainly likely that many others who make these connections don't shift into Fundamental Wellbeing. Most likely only a tiny percentage do, and it may not be different than the number who would transition otherwise.

Why might a personal connection make a difference, especially if the person is just saying the same things s / he has written? An obvious answer is that the Finder can take in detailed personal information, and respond accordingly. Rather than getting a generic message, a personalized version is received. The Finder may also use a teaching method that requires interaction. For example, some employ a method that digs deeply into your beliefs and ideologies.

There could also be more to the story than this type of conscious interaction. For decades, researchers have been attempting to control for 'experimenter effects' in human research. These are unintentional biases and influences that get introduced into academic research by the scientists designing and carrying it out. There are a bewildering number of variables that should be controlled in order to conduct a 'valid' experiment.

Even in a strictly controlled laboratory environment, information can be accidentally and unintentionally conveyed though actions, voice, and so forth. Much of this is not under conscious control. Influences extend to hidden and rarely considered mechanisms, such as chemical-level signaling. A good example is the exchange of pheromones between people.

Given the high number of information transfer types and mechanisms across virtually all forms of human-to-human interaction, there has been no way for our research project to examine more than a handful in relation to Fundamental Wellbeing. Their degree of influence in producing a shift remains unknown. There could be any number of 'hidden' influences that make it a good idea for someone who wants to transition to visit with a Finder.

This is not to suggest that you need to go meet a Finder if you want to experience Fundamental Wellbeing. Many participants had no known connections to one prior to their shift. It's also important to consider that all Finders are not the same. If there is something to a personal connection, it is possible that you may need to locate a Finder that is the 'right fit' for you in order to benefit from the interaction. Remember, most of these individuals seem to have no effect on their families and friends. And, there are plenty of people who have flocked to Finders but still don't experience Fundamental Wellbeing.

Meetings with Finders often appear synchronistic. In fact, increased feelings of synchronicity have been tied to the experience of Fundamental Wellbeing for nearly as long as it has been reported. In the next chapter, we look at the impact that being a Finder has on synchronicity and flow—and once again discover that many of the common beliefs about these topics are off the mark.

CHAPTER 32: SYNCHRONICITY AND FLOW

Some religious and spiritual traditions suggest that experiencing Fundamental Wellbeing literally changes the way the world interacts with Finders. At the extreme, these traditions propose that the external world shifts to become harmonious, to ensure their perfect ongoing health, and even to fulfill whatever they desire. While these concepts are undoubtedly a form of 'spiritual salesmanship,' this does not mean they are entirely without merit.

Let's start with some simple facts and observations. There are Finders across every location on the continuum who are in failing health. Some of these health problems result from typical aging, but certainly not all. On a more basic level, many wear glasses, need or have needed dental work, and have other typical health issues. And, some have died since they were interviewed. In fact, some of the individuals who were regarded as among the most advanced from their religious or spiritual tradition reached out to participate in our research just prior to their death, knowing that they were going to die soon from a specific health condition. The idea that Fundamental Wellbeing transforms an individual into a perfect picture of health, makes them live forever, and so forth is not supported either overall, or for any location on the continuum that the project has researched thus far.

A related idea is synchronistic support. This means that events and other manifestations happen at just the right time to fulfill a desire or need, sometimes quite improbably. Some traditions directly state that all events in a Finder's life will flow optimally and wonderfully. There seem to be as many examples as there are people who want things. Major categories include: the nature of close relationships, sufficient wealth to live comfortably, remaining free to live your life, and so forth.

Here again, the facts don't seem to support the idea of synchronistic support for all Finders. They still lose spouses, children, and others close to them. They get divorced. They go to jail or have close family members go to jail. They suffer significant financial losses, up to and including being left destitute at times in their lives when they are old and have no other means of support. All of these examples, and many others, have been directly observed during the research. Fundamental Wellbeing does not seem to magically make the world support you in an optimum way, even when someone is from a tradition that promises this will be the case when the person reaches a certain level—and the person has reached that level or beyond it.

Getting beyond this obvious surface level, many Finders do report experiencing their lives as more synchronistic. At a basic level, the present-moment focus that accompanies Fundamental Wellbeing seems to bring an increased feeling of synchronicity, including the sense that more supportive events occur. How this is interpreted often relates to their continuum location. Synchronicity can also play a role in the transition to Fundamental Wellbeing.

Recall that a minority of Finders gradually phase into Fundamental Wellbeing, rather than having it arrive in one moment. Synchronicity is often reported to have increased for these individuals just prior to and during their transition. This makes them feel supported and encourages them to keep going until they have fully shifted. It also plays a role as Finders deepen into Fundamental Wellbeing.

Once they experience Fundamental Wellbeing, for some, synchronicity is noted passively. Not much focus is put on it. For others, it becomes a key component of their belief system. This is even true for Finders who claim they don't have a belief system. Those in Location 2 often judge whether they are "on path" or "off path" based on the amount of synchronistic flow being experienced. They use it like a type of feedback communication system, constantly testing the world with actions and examining the results for the appearance of synchronistic support.

JOY, LOVE, AND THE DIVINE AS INDICATORS

Joy is another common indicator that is used as feedback by some in Locations 2 and 3. When a decision needs to be made, Finders might try to imagine or "feel into" the possible choices, looking for the one that brings up the most joy in them. This sense of joy is often associated with increased feelings of synchronistic support for these individuals. Others use love or a sense of the divine in a similar way.

Having spent a great deal of time around Finders, anecdotally I can attest to having seen what appeared to be some amazing flows of synchronicity. I've experienced many impressive and improbable events arise just as they were needed. I've also witnessed individuals who seemed to get amazing results by trying to actively follow joy and listen for the synchronistic feedback from these decisions.

Sometimes, I've been party to this type of joy / synchronicity feedback for weeks at a time. During these periods, I've also witnessed times where nothing seemed to be working out. For Finders who believe in this, prolonged 'failure' periods are typically viewed as just a type of feedback, not something that might suggest an issue with their belief system.

During these "off" periods, some Finders have a tendency to attribute the lack of synchronicity to others around them. These Finders are generally quite sensitive to, and judgmental of, the lack of synchronistic flow in other people's lives. They usually are not as forgiving with others as they are with themselves when things don't seem to be working out.

SURRENDER AS A STRATEGY

An alternative strategy of synchronicity and flow generation that Finders use is trying to just surrender to the ongoing flow of life, no matter what is happening. It's easy to see where this comes from, as it elegantly combines several core aspects of Fundamental Wellbeing. The strategy rests on being centered in the present moment, and its sense of underlying perfection. The tendency within Fundamental Wellbeing to be non-judgmental also combines with the changes Finders experience in the reduction or elimination of self-referential thought and increasing distance from emotion.

Each of these are, essentially, taken to the max, with the goal typically being to surrender to the present moment without any psychological triggers arising. For some, this means both positive and negative psychological triggers, and pursuing an ever more stable form of psychological equilibrium. This strategy is especially popular with Finders who seek to ferret out and extinguish as much of their former psychological conditioning as they can find. Not all go in this direction, but for the Finders who do, surrender often becomes a life path and belief system in itself.

Overall, strong support for synchronistic beliefs has not been directly supported in the research. To be definitive about this, the total population of Finders in at least one country or region would need to be well known and sampled in a precise and systematic way. Things are a long way from that, so it's important to keep in mind that these are anecdotal research impressions. From our experience, however, Finders seem to have things work out and not work out, just like others. They live in a wide range of environments and circumstances, despite and often in spite of their beliefs. It's not uncommon, for example, for a Finder who just had his house foreclosed on to continue to fully embrace their flow and synchronistic belief systems.

One specific example involves a later-location individual who is deeply steeped in a belief system involving synchronistic flow for Finders. For him it originated in his Hindu-based religion. Like many with this belief, he has a set of key examples from his life that seem to support it. Because this person is a long-time research participant, I was able to watch this process occur step-by-step.

He had been fighting to maintain his property for some time when we first met. Over our subsequent research interviews, he would fill me in and keep me up-to-date on what was happening. At each meeting, there seemed to be a new hurdle in the process to keep his home. Once, one of these even unfolded on the day I was there. Each time, he expressed what seemed like an unwavering belief that flow would see this hurdle working out, and the whole thing would finally be over. Ultimately, he lost his home, which led to a suboptimal period of time in his life. As he put it, "the last couple of years could have been a lot easier if that hadn't happened."

Despite every setback, to this day he maintains the same belief system involving the support Finders receive in the form of synchronicity and flow. He is highly intelligent, and freely acknowledges that experiences like this are somewhat perplexing, but the absolute certainty in these beliefs remains. This might sound remarkable, but most humans seem to have a built-in mechanism for belief despite the actual evidence. In this sense, although they usually insist otherwise, Finders are no different than the rest of the population.

In Location 4 and beyond, the absence of agency can make every moment seem synchronistic. It feels as though everything is just emerging; every word and action, as well as everything else in their environment. This may be where some of the more extreme lore around synchronicity originated.

WISH FULFILLMENT

A related topic is being able to "wish" or "intend" for events to happen and have them manifest. Some Finders describe the ability to do this. These individuals relate fantastic stories that run the range of Western human desires, including medical miracles, perfect families, wealth, and so forth. These Finders also often claim to be able to manifest in others' lives as well, and even for humanity as a whole. Generally, they say that belief is the key.

Their hypothesis is that if you believe something is possible, it actually is. These individuals have often meticulously experimented with this over many years. Fundamental Wellbeing is often viewed as a key element in making this work. There are a variety of beliefs about why, but most center on an importance of being released from personal desires and / or being in greater alignment with deeper levels of reality.

Which brings us to many people's favorite topic: sex. One thing that it seems virtually no one wants to manifest in order to transition into Fundamental Wellbeing is celibacy. Good news, and maybe not so good news, lies ahead.

CHAPTER 33: SEX AND FUNDAMENTAL WELLBEING

Some religious and spiritual traditions suggest that abstaining from sex assists with the transition into Fundamental Wellbeing. A few even go so far as to insist that it's required. There has been no indication of either in the data so far, but there have been interesting findings regarding sexuality. Finders' sex lives represent a cross section of what is found in the general population. Depending on someone's preferences, this might include: sex with one or more partners (of one or more gender), masturbation, sexual fantasies, the bodily experience of sexual attraction, so-called fetishes like dominance and submission, and more.

Many Finders experience changes in their sexuality. This includes everything from an increased sex drive, to a total loss of it. The effects can be temporary, or have persisted since their transition into Fundamental Wellbeing. Changes can also take place when a Finder shifts between locations on the continuum.

By far the most common change involves routine sexual practices and patterns. It's common for partners in long-term relationships to learn what each other likes, and establish routines. Once someone transitions, new exploration typically arises. The previous preferences aren't forgotten or ignored, but a new cycle of discovery develops and the old patterns get updated.

Finders view this as positive, and all parties seem to enjoy the results. It is possible that the old habits were tied to aspects of the Narrative-Self that are simply no longer present, or strong. The changes may also relate to the heightened sensory experiences and increased present-moment awareness that arrive with Fundamental Wellbeing.

There doesn't seem to be a strong relationship between specific sexual changes and continuum location, except at Location 4. Here, Finders are much more likely to report a temporary loss of their sex drive. As unappealing as that may sound, this location can also produce a dramatic and positive transformation in the other direction.

A paraphrase of the sexual upside that can arrive with Location 4 for a single Finder might be, "The first time I had sex after the transition occurred, it was amazing. Simply amazing. Unlike anything I'd experienced. When that relationship ended, I was thinking that I would really miss the great sex! But, then it was the same with the next person, and the next. It wasn't the person!"

For these Finders, sexual frequency often increases, as can their number of partners. It's not uncommon for women in this situation to use terms like "promiscuous" to describe their sexuality post-transition. Men do not use similar labels, though they seem to equally apply.

Location 4 Finders who experience this in committed relationships are equally fortunate. This new sensory pleasure often combines with the renewed exploration to dramatically increase satisfaction with their partner. The project has not seen evidence that it makes a committed Finder more promiscuous; however, Fundamental Wellbeing does not exempt people from having affairs.

DEEPER URGES EMERGE

Many people have suppressed sexual urges. The feelings of certainty, truth, and perfection that arrive with Fundamental Wellbeing can combine to make Finders feel more at ease with expressing their sexuality. This is the case even if it runs contrary to strong societal taboos, and even the law.

For example, growing up in a culture that penalizes same sex relationships might lead to stifling one's attraction for the same sex. Some participants discussed living a heterosexual lifestyle prior to experiencing Fundamental Wellbeing. Afterwards, they became openly homosexual or bisexual, even when there were serious societal consequences. Most of these Finders had been repressing or hiding their sexual preferences for some time. A small number said they were not attracted to members of the same sex prior to experiencing Fundamental Wellbeing.

Related to this are types of sex that are sometimes considered alternative, and even 'deviant,' by society, such as sadomasochism, dominance and submission, and similar 'fetishes.' Some Finders discussed their involvement in these types of sexual activity. A tiny minority even shared how learning to surrender as a submissive brought on experiences that culminated in the transition to Fundamental Wellbeing. Other Finders who experimented with this type of sexuality found that it suppressed their experience of Fundamental Wellbeing. For some, it triggered conditioning and pushed it down. For others, it activated dormant parts of the Narrative-Self.

Just as in the real world, now that we've covered sex, it's time to talk marriage (and divorce). In the next chapter, you'll see what happens when Finders and non-Finders hook up, when one partner transitions out of the blue in an established relationship, and more. You'll also learn about top causes of divorce among Finders, and what can be done to prevent it.

CHAPTER 34: COMMITTED RELATIONSHIPS AND DIVORCE

This chapter discusses committed relationships between two individuals, when one or both of them experience Fundamental Wellbeing. While other sections of the book have touched sporadically on this topic, its importance warrants a dedicated and detailed discussion. Family relationships can be among the most challenging aspects of Fundamental Wellbeing. The pages that follow include the most important things we've learned about how to strengthen them.

Many Finders are or have been in a committed relationship. Some of these relationships started prior to Fundamental Wellbeing, some after. Some have been short-term, others long-term. Some involved marriage, others did not. A healthy percentage involved families with children, and even grandchildren and great-grandchildren. In some instances, the children were from only one of the partners, who may or may not have been Finders.

Not all relationships fall into the standard 'nuclear family'-type arrangement. As with the general population, many medium and long-term relationships did not involve marriage. Some, both married and not, weren't monogamous on the part of the Finder, his or her partner, or both. The research also encountered monogamous and non-monogamous homosexual relationships of varying lengths, including very long-term ones. This included homosexual relationships where both partners were Finders.

TRANSITIONING WHILE IN A RELATIONSHIP

It is not uncommon for someone to become a Finder while married or in another form of committed relationship. If both partners were pursuing Fundamental Wellbeing, the transition of one partner can cause jealousy in the relationship. This is especially true if the partner who shifted wasn't originally interested in Fundamental Wellbeing, and the other partner had been pursuing it for some time.

This jealousy is rare, though, and the most common outcome is mutual support. The non-Finder now has someone close at hand to speak with and get advice from. The Finder has someone they can confide in and be supported by through their transition and beyond.

Sometimes both partners become Finders in less than a year. Most times in our research population, their transition was years apart. Once both partners experience Fundamental Wellbeing, it typically strengthens the couple's relationship, though there are times when it contributes to divorce.

For example, some couples have long-lasting friction between them that they view as positive. These individuals often believe it is important to their pursuit of Fundamental Wellbeing to uncover triggers to work on, and other ways to "grow." After they both transition, any remaining friction suppresses the experience of Fundamental Wellbeing. It's not uncommon for one of them to seek a divorce if this friction remains for too long.

AN UNSUPPORTIVE PARTNER

Many who pursue Fundamental Wellbeing have partners that are ambivalent or even outright against it. Often, one of the first things a new Finder does is discuss their transition with immediate family. These initial discussions can go poorly, but proper planning can help. Most commonly, the unsupportive family members express concern and cut the conversation short. The matter is dropped entirely, and everyone pretends it never happened.

These exchanges can be delicate, and counter-productive for all involved. They can easily give a non-Finder serious concerns about his or her partner's mental health. Even worse, if the non-Finder has a conflicting religious or spiritual belief, deeply held existential concerns can be raised.

It seems best for newly minted Finders to gently test the waters. The initial conversation should be just with a spouse or partner, and not the entire family. If it doesn't go well, it might be best to just drop it and not mention it for a while. However, once the topic is broached it will remain on everyone's mind, and a conversation will eventually occur. Being persistent in the face of strict opposition can land a Finder on the receiving end of worried calls from other family members and friends, prayer interdictions, and in the most extreme cases even forced psychological treatment.

There are many examples of partners with different religious or spiritual beliefs coming to an understanding. Typically, this comes from careful planning that begins well before Fundamental Wellbeing. It's important to lay the conceptual groundwork. Sharing reading materials and videos about Fundamental Wellbeing is often a great place to start. In the best circumstances, this can be followed up by going to Fundamental Wellbeing related events, arranging meetings with other Finders, and so forth. Except on rare occasions, this 'easing in' strategy seems to work with even the most hostile partner. It is less effective, though, if the partner is highly dogmatic in his or her spiritual or religious beliefs, and feels that Fundamental Wellbeing can never be compatible with them.

In these cases, the most effective tactic seems to be a Finder deeply immersing him or herself in the partner's religion, while simultaneously taking an interest in its mystical side. This strategy must be pursued gently and with caution, because mainstream versions of the major religions often view their mystical aspects unfavorably. However, because it works within the partner's belief system rather than against it, this type of strategy does seem to produce openings for sharing and understanding that may not exist otherwise.

Occasionally, one of two highly religious individuals who are living and worshipping together has a surprise shift into Fundamental Wellbeing. It's common for each partner to have very little knowledge, if any, of the mystical aspects of their religion. This can produce a significant disruption in their relationship.

In the best circumstance, the partners will pull together and take a combined interest in understanding what happened and how it can best be supported. Sometimes there is an initial adjustment period where they try to determine if the change was from a 'good source,' so to speak. Once they are comfortable that it is, they form a united and supportive front.

As the above suggests, a partner doesn't have to be familiar with, or even believe in, Fundamental Wellbeing to be supportive. Those who don't feel personally attracted to it can still be sympathetic and caring. These individuals will often pick up information about it from their partner as s / he studies, and seek to deepen their understanding. Some even go on to pursue it.

ISOLATED FINDERS VS. COMMUNAL FINDERS

There can be a significant difference between Finders who are routinely around other Finders, and those who are not. Most Finders transition to Fundamental Wellbeing in relative isolation. At best, they might know one or two other Finders, who may not even live near them.

As mentioned previously, the transition to Fundamental Wellbeing can lead to strongly held ideas and beliefs. A Finder's noetic sense can be extremely powerful, and in isolation this usually increases over time. As a result, they tend to give strong preference to their own views versus others.

For Finders who live more closely in community with other Finders, this is rarely the case. Unless they live in a dogmatic religious or spiritual community, the atmosphere is often one of greater understanding, acceptance, and mutual exploration. These Finders have usually come to accept that their noetic sense can be very different from other Finders, and they do not automatically assume it is the most accurate. They also have other Finders providing them with observations and feedback on their thoughts, beliefs, actions, and so on. When non-Finders do this, it usually rings hollow, but it is not as easy to dismiss coming from other Finders. This further takes the edge off their views and beliefs.

Being in a relationship with an isolated Finder versus a more communal one is often a night and day difference. In many ways, just like other Finders, the person will be far more flexible, understanding, and supportive than most other partners. Fundamental Wellbeing does bring a significant amount of openness and tolerance along with it.

However, a Finder who deepens in isolation from other Finders will often develop some extreme cases of inflexibility regarding what is right and wrong for him or her across a range of essential issues that can make things very difficult for the other person in the relationship. It's not uncommon for such a Finder to insist that the other person needs to "grow" in specific ways for the relationship to be harmonious. What the Finder is really saying is that, "it's my way or the highway," and the person genuinely means it. Generally, this situation does not lead to thriving relationships unless the other person does choose to change and bend to the Finder's will.

When two Finders are in the relationship, at least one of whom has been isolated during their development of Fundamental Wellbeing, it often comes down to how alike the Finders views and beliefs are. If they are similar, it can lead to a very strong relationship, unless one of them significantly changes later. If not, it can make for a difficult time together. As mentioned previously, some Finders view these difficulties as opportunities for psychological conditioning to arise and get extinguished, however that can be problematic out long-term. Even with a belief system that prioritizes deconditioning, eventually ongoing conflict becomes undesirable. By far the best relationships are both with and between Finders who have spent plenty of time around other Finders.

When these Finders come together to form a committed relationship, it is often amazing how much respect and deep appreciation the partners seem to have for each other. Finders in most continuum locations appear to be able to develop deeply supportive and caring bonds. Even in the further locations, where personal, or even all, emotion is absent, they seem capable of forming deep and meaningful relationships with each other.

FUNDAMENTAL WELLBEING AND DIVORCE

Just as with the general population, Finder marriages can end with divorce. This includes marriages involving two Finders. The cultural and religious expectations that cause some couples to remain together when they might otherwise split usually have less effect on these individuals.

179

Even deeply devout Finders from religions that look unfavorably upon divorce don't seem as constrained by this dogma. This includes individuals who situate their experience of Fundamental Wellbeing almost solely within their religion and its tenets. Finders are also less prone to remain in a relationship for the "sake of the children." Although this is a consideration, it does not dominate their decision, even when it is considered very important within their culture.

The two main culprits for divorce are: having the feeling of inner peace "pushed down," as mentioned in an earlier chapter, and the difficulty of living with a partner who cannot return feelings of personal love. Recall that the former involved the suppression of inner peace and wellbeing by emotional triggers. And, that many of these triggers are produced within a Finder's family life.

When getting some distance from the family allows inner peace and wellbeing to remain high, some Finders choose to live separately. This generally happens shortly after an individual transitions into Fundamental Wellbeing. Of course, the other option is for the Finder to stick it out and let as many of these triggers as possible extinguish over time. Most in the research study chose the latter. Years down the road, Finders who chose both of these directions seemed completely fine with their decisions.

The other primary cause of divorce among Finders relates to the later continuum locations. By Location 3, emotions are less personal. An easy way to visualize this might be to think about your personal love for someone, and then God's love for that person. Someone grounded in Location 3 has love that tends more towards the latter. Even though their love for their partner is not personal, they are so outwardly loving and caring that the person usually cannot tell. It only becomes a problem if discussed, and their partner cannot deal with the idea of it. Location 3 individuals can make amazing partners, especially if their Fundamental Wellbeing deepening did not occur in isolation.

At Location 4 there is typically no experience of emotion. It's easy to understand how this might cause relationship problems. While the Finder feels a deep sense of completeness, his or her partner still has a Narrative-Self that thrives on external validation. 'Normal' committed relationships are, in part, about a partner's personal love providing that validation. Finding yourself with a partner who no longer experiences any form of love can be very difficult. In these instances, it's often the non-Finder who ends the relationship.

As you might suspect, this is not just a problem for existing relationships. Location 4 individuals can have difficulty finding and building committed personal relationships. No matter how wonderful things seem to start, the absence of love tends to cause the other person to drift away. One option is to find another Location 4 or later individual, but their scarcity makes that difficult.

Some manage to find partners whose Narrative-Self is less dependent on getting personal love from their partner, though this is also rare. In most cases, Location 4 Finders either remain alone or learn how to respond appropriately so that their partner feels loved. They often get exceptionally good at this, because their own emotions aren't influencing the situation.

As we've seen in this chapter, peace, or the disturbance of it, is often of utmost importance to the success of Finders' committed relationships. That's actually just the tip of the iceberg. The reality is that peace is the benchmark and guiding force for virtually all areas of a Finder's life, as we'll see next.

CHAPTER 35: IT'S (MOSTLY) ABOUT PEACE

If you'd heard about Fundamental Wellbeing before reading this book, you were probably attracted by some of the 'spiritual salesmanship' around it. Maybe you were drawn to the notion of uncovering "ultimate truth." Or possibly it was obtaining super powers, like reliable psychic abilities, that could give you an undisputed edge in life. Or maybe it was the dream of permanently ending all suffering in your life and experiencing a flow where the universe just seemed to magically support you and never give you a rough time. Perhaps it was all of this and more.

With those things put into their proper context at this point, you may be wondering what makes Fundamental Wellbeing so great. Why is it that the vast majority of people who experience it say that they wouldn't trade it for anything? What is really, truly, at the heart of it?

The answer is very simple: in large part, Fundamental Wellbeing is about peace. A very special kind of peace settles in as part of the transition, and is the part of the experience that most people say they'd never want to part with. In fact, post-transition living largely comes down to Finders navigating their relationship to it.

This peace has been covered many times, from many different angles, over the course of this book. The simplest way to sum it up is that the peace is what replaces its opposite, fundamental discontentment, when that disappears. Examining the average person's relationship to fundamental discontentment speaks volumes about how a Finder navigates their relationship to peace.

If you stop and truly examine the average person's life, it becomes obvious that it comes down to tradeoffs that are being made to mitigate their fundamental discontentment. It's the foundation that all of their experience is built upon, and they spend a great deal of their time and energy trying to pacify it. People will do almost anything to get as much distance from it as possible.

Sometimes they make the decision that the best option is pleasure in the moment. Other times, they might sacrifice for what they perceive to be a more substantial or durable gain in the future. Every moment involves a carefully calculated move in an overall strategy to minimize fundamental discontentment.

Finders have this discontentment replaced with a deep-seated, foundational, inner peace. Just like the discontentment is for others, this peace simply seems to be there. However, also just like discontentment, there are things that can pull it closer or create some distance to it. The inner game for Finders is about this peace, though some miss this because of their former habit of focusing on and managing discontentment.

THE FINDERS' NEW GAME

A Finder's life is ultimately about their relationship to this newly found peace. Every choice and action is weighed, consciously and unconsciously, against the impact that it will have on inner peace. Peace is prized above all else, but life brings caveats.

Some things need to be done. For example, a Finder might be in a financial situation that seems inescapable. Even if s/he wanted to, it might seem impossible to simply leave it all behind and go off to deepen in Fundamental Wellbeing. Most Finders have forced choices like this in their lives, things that lead them to make what seem like necessary tradeoffs that lessen the amount of peace they could otherwise experience.

Other things are clearly optional choices. One example of this was a Finder who had decided to stay with his spouse of fifty years, but who also made it clear to friends and family that if she ever died, he would most likely never be seen or heard from again. Examples like this are fascinating, because they show a clear value judgment is being made. For this person, obligations to children and grandchildren can be met and moved on from, however his or her spouse seemed to be a durable commitment until death—even though there is no question that moving away from this spouse would lead to deeper peace.

A topic like this, and the values around it for Finders, can be quite nuanced. Subsequent interviews with this participant revealed that both his mother and mother-in-law had severe dementia at the time of her death, and his sister-in-law died young from early onset Alzheimer's. Being present through their journeys into death led him to a surprising additional decision about his wife. He'd decided that if she ever went thirty days without recognizing his face or being able to remember his name, he would pay to put her in a high-end care facility and continue his journey along the continuum in isolation.

During the research it became clear that most Finders' decisions and actions are driven by their values, even if some insist adamantly that this is not the case. This fact might be one reason that many religious and spiritual systems place such weight on instilling the values they want Finders to have while they are still on the path and haven't yet transitioned. Of course, values can and do change over time. Certainly most people, including the person from the example above, were not raised thinking it was okay to walk away from their children and grandchildren. In fact, it could be argued that people generally feel more personal responsibility to their offspring than their spouse. However, in this case, over many years of being in Fundamental Wellbeing, this person has had these values reverse.

Natural tendencies also seem to play a role for Finders. Those who were very strong extroverts prior to their transition often have that tendency remain. As discussed, it's common for Finders to want to be around people less as they deepen, and to prefer to be around other Finders when they do seek company. However, strong extroverts can buck this trend. They can continue to be fed by interactions with people, their stories, and so on. This is especially true if they transitioned while young, and their extroverted tendencies grew alongside their deepening into Fundamental Wellbeing. It's almost as if they are deeply wired in a different way that Fundamental Wellbeing adapts to and accommodates. There are limits, of course, and if they want to embark on the Path of Freedom instead of the Path of Humanity, even these individuals will increasingly isolate themselves.

So, life as a Finder seems to primarily relate to a balancing of elements. Things that they believe absolutely must be done for survival (as long as survival is desired), things that are driven by their core values, and things that are dictated by deeper aspects of their nature—all in service to what produces the most peace, and most importantly, what does not jeopardize Fundamental Wellbeing. The obvious next question involves if there is an ultimate form of this peace, and Fundamental Wellbeing in general.

CHAPTER 36: IS THERE AN ULTIMATE FORM OF FUNDAMENTAL WELLBEING?

Among those who have known about and been interested in Fundamental Wellbeing, the question the research team hears most is, "What is the ultimate form?" Usually these are religious or spiritually inclined individuals who arrive with some kind of bias drawn from the views of the tradition or traditions they have studied. The diversity of opinions on this topic is confusing to most people. As you might imagine, given the breadth and amount of data collected over the course of this project, the research team definitely experienced the same. Ultimately, people often settle for a person's or a system's opinion that they are most comfortable with. Below is the one this project has led to, though it comes with a strong caveat that, probably, no one really knows the answer to this question.

Whether there is an 'ultimate' form of Fundamental Wellbeing for you most likely depends upon what you are after. Some religious and spiritual systems that have Fundamental Wellbeing at their heart primarily believe that it should be maximally cultivated in certain ways to ensure an optimum life after this one. The Western, Abrahamic traditions like Christianity and Islam have mystical traditions that generally gravitate towards Location 3. Some Eastern traditions also stop around this point, while others stop earlier at Location 2 or advocate going to Location 4. Still other Eastern traditions push the envelope even further. They recommend extraordinary sacrifices in terms of how one spends life, in an effort to optimize what comes after it. Generally, their belief is to go as far as you can on the Path of Freedom.

The contrary view is to optimize Fundamental Wellbeing for this life. For these individuals, notions of something after death can enter the picture, but these thoughts aren't the major driver. Rather, it comes down to integrating Fundamental Wellbeing in ways that allow you to lead the best life possible now. Many of these individuals figure that this will contribute positively to whatever is next, if anything.

The research didn't reveal any clear-cut answers about what the ultimate form of Fundamental Wellbeing might be. Certainly, it seems tempting to believe the very far locations on the Path of Freedom might be it. However, people who experience these are so rare that it seems impossible to know at present. And, it appears that these further reaches of Fundamental Wellbeing are nearly unimaginable for the average person to reach. They also seem quite out of phase with anything approaching a normal life that allows one to have a job, raise a family, and so on. Does this mean that these distant locations are what the average person should be pursuing? That doesn't seem likely.

CHOOSING YOUR ULTIMATE LOCATION

The 'ultimate' answer for you probably depends mostly on two things. The first is which one of the two options you decide to believe. Is Fundamental Wellbeing primarily about this life, or an assumed afterlife of some kind? For the most part, the research team members have leaned towards the former, but that no doubt relates to our own cultural and scientific conditioning. Really, you're on your own for this one.

The second is what is most appropriate for your life. In the West, across many religious, philosophical, and spiritual systems, a 'take it to the max' approach is often advocated involving Fundamental Wellbeing, though granted with a wide range of locations as recommended end-points. Our research has seen that this is rarely the best idea for someone's life. Some locations are more suited to specific living situations than others. Even Location 3, as amazing as it feels, has caused issues for people. For example, more than one manager or executive who participated in the research has noted that shifting into it made them much more prone to generosity than being a good steward of the company's resources. While nice for employees, vendors, and others in the short term, that is probably not so great for the longer-term survivability of the company.

CHAPTER 37: CLOSING PERSONAL THOUGHTS

Because of the claims they made, I began this project expecting to find that individuals who experience Fundamental Wellbeing were delusional, self-deceptive, or pathological in some way. From a normal psychological standpoint, their claims seemed too amazing to be true. No matter how hard we looked, I couldn't find this among the vast majority of the population we studied. Over time, slowly, painstakingly, and even reluctantly, I came to accept as true what Finders told us about how they experienced the world, and the ramifications that came with it.

Prior to this project, I'd never experienced anything even remotely like what the participants talked about. I had never taken hallucinogenic drugs or had any kind of peak or mystical experience. My youthful cries to God seemed to always go unanswered. Looking back, I think this was a key factor in the success this project enjoyed. I simply had no idea what I would find, and so it was a ground up, skeptical investigation. Most of the other academics who have explored these topics did so because they were seeking to understand experiences they'd had, or beliefs they held.

As the years rolled on, it became increasingly clear that Fundamental Wellbeing was something that I definitely wanted to experience. After interfacing with nearly a thousand people by that point, I had a pretty good idea of how to do it, but decided to hold off. My outsider's viewpoint seemed too important to the project's data collection. Eventually, the day came when major data collection and analysis had finished, and I decided to allow myself to slip over into it.

As others have said, it truly is beyond great. It's the thing you've spent your whole life looking for without knowing it, as you search in so many other countless and fruitless directions. I'm profoundly grateful for it and, as so many others told me, cannot imagine that I would trade it for anything.

At the same time, I cannot count the number of times I've seen the transition to Fundamental Wellbeing dramatically disrupt people's lives. From bankrupting the previously rich to destroying what seemed like very well-established and happy marriages and families, some of the damage done has been far reaching. Our research has suggested that this largely has one thing in common: reaching for forms of Fundamental Wellbeing that are not optimally aligned with current life circumstances. Because of this, I'm choosing to end this book with a personal voice, a personal opinion, and a personal plea.

In my opinion, if you don't already experience it, you should definitely give Fundamental Wellbeing a try. For those of us who live in it, going back is truly unthinkable. Every now and then, I try a new technology that stimulates my brain and accidentally knocks me out of it. Fortunately, the effect has always been temporary. Those brief glimpses of what was once normal, but can now only be described as hellish, drive me on to do all I can to help others have safe, effective, reliable, and accessible ways to reach Fundamental Wellbeing, and to provide the information they need to adjust optimally to it.

Ultimately Fundamental Wellbeing is just one part of lived experience. Many other things also matter. People who pursue Fundamental Wellbeing often do so to the exclusion of other important and amazing aspects of life. Given that historically very few who pursue it actually get there, it makes sense to question this strategy.

Over the course of this research, I've met scores of people who were very old and spent a great deal of their life trying to reach Fundamental Wellbeing, unsuccessfully. Their experience was filled with such sorrow over all they passed up, that it was hard not to be deeply touched. These individuals have filled my inbox almost since the project's inception in hopes that we could help improve their odds.

The zealousness that it often takes to reach Fundamental Wellbeing frequently carries on after it. This is where some of the 'take it to the max' approaches enter the picture. Here again, a caution. As I write this, I doubt that anyone on Earth has had more in-depth, life-probing sit-downs with Finders than I have. It's been thousands at this point for well over a decade. Essentially, my days are filled mostly with Finders. I've seen literally countless examples of people who pushed themselves as hard as they could trying to maximize Fundamental Wellbeing, and wound up ruining key aspects of the rest of their life in the process.

While it is true that often these Finders say that the internal place they reached is worth it, the reality is that our research has shown that *any* form of Fundamental Wellbeing is a great way to experience life. Pushing hard may have shifted them into further locations, but if I'd done the same interview in one of their previous locations, they would have told me that things were awesome there, too. And, that location wouldn't have wreaked havoc on their finances, family, or other key aspects of their lives. I know this from having watched varying scenarios play out in our long-term research subjects.

Remember, there have been countless ideas about how far to push the envelope. Every known location has Finders who advocated it as the desired endpoint to reach. Which begs the question, is it really so important to reach Location X? Is it truly worth upending other incredible parts of your life to reach a goal merely because another Finder or Finder-based tradition says you should?

Perhaps the number one thing I've learned from all of this research is that, as a Finder, you should carefully consider all of the contents of this book and what actually matches your life. Consider what your family needs. Consider your wider responsibilities. Consider other aspects of your quality of life and what will contribute most to them. If you're in a location where it seems like that isn't possible—because it feels like you can't take action, make a decision, and so on—just allow these words to be read, and see what your brain makes of them.

Yes, Fundamental Wellbeing is awesome. Yes, the peace that arrives with it is a pressing internal priority. But, don't forget to take others into account so you can lead a well-balanced life as well, and be as much of a blessing to those you touch with it as possible.

Peace.

EPILOGUE: THE FUTURE OF FUNDAMENTAL WELLBEING

Until now, there haven't been that many paths into Fundamental Wellbeing. For some, it just happens. Something clicks in their brain, rewiring happens, and presto!...they're a Finder. For others, it happens from the depths of depression. Still others actively pursue it with meditation and similar methods.

All of these paths are relatively organic, meaning they most likely involve natural tendencies that already reside in the brain. Certain forms of Buddhism, for example, guide people down very precise methodological paths that they expect will lead to Fundamental Wellbeing for at least some of them. Essentially, they seem to have found methods that work with natural processes in the brain that lead to this or that location on the continuum.

While that's great, the downside has been the unreliability of these systems. They work for some, but certainly not for most. People's brains are highly variable. For many years now, the project focused on traditional, psychological, and alternative paths to Fundamental Wellbeing, including technological ones.

These days, we expect certain things. One of these is for life to be made easier by science and technology. Most people feel too busy to sit and meditate for a meaningful amount of time each day, much less keep it up for years. Even if meditation systems work extremely well, this fact alone is a huge limiter on the impact Fundamental Wellbeing can make today.

This is the age of pills and push buttons, and one of these is most likely going to be needed for large numbers of people to experience Fundamental Wellbeing, decide if it is right for them, and ease their integration into it. As a technologist and neuroscientist, for me this means focusing on finding a button people can press. To date, the project has worked its way through every practical brain feedback and stimulation technology, hoping to find a match. The problem is that research up to this point has revealed that most of the regions related to Fundamental Wellbeing in the brain are very deep, and this makes them hard to reach with existing technology.

There is one promising technology that is being explored, *transcranial focused ultrasound* (FUS). This is just a fancy term for a device that uses sound to modulate the brain noninvasively through the skull. It's the first technology that can reach deeply in and mostly just effect the areas that need to be targeted. As this book goes to press, it's expensive and there are only a handful of people in the world you'd want to entrust your brain to who know how to use it. Fortunately, many of them work or collaborate with us, and it is showing great promise.

This type of technology opens up an interesting new vista for Fundamental Wellbeing. Unlike everything else, FUS is not a 'natural' method. It uses sound waves from outside your head to directly modulate activity in the brain. It's very likely that it will break the mold when it comes to Fundamental Wellbeing. It may even make much of what you're reading in this book obsolete.

The ability to activate or reduce activity in regions of the brain that are associated with Fundamental Wellbeing has already been shown using neurofeedback, mostly in research-grade functional magnetic resonance imaging scanners. This can involve something as simple as a research participant lying in the scanner, looking at a bar on a screen and trying to make it go up or down.

That bar is linked via software to an area of the brain using complex real-time neuroimaging. When the bar goes down, for example, it can be because it has been programmed to show that activity in a certain area of the brain is decreasing. It's a way for people to directly train regions of the brain that are relevant to Fundamental Wellbeing. Unfortunately, this isn't widely available because the equipment used is rare, expensive, and requires a highly skilled operator and support staff.

However, it's likely that the same effect can be created by directly up or down regulating brain regions with direct brain stimulation. It may even be as simple as someone just having to sit there and experience it.

In this scenario, one or more small devices are placed against the skull, and everything happens with the push of a button.

So, why could this be a game changer when it comes to Fundamental Wellbeing? Right now, it seems as though we are all at the mercy of the brain's responses to methods like meditation. A lot has gone into figuring these out, but ultimately they are just using natural tendencies in the brain. When these work, the brain seems to organize itself into experiences that take the form of Locations 1, 2, and so on. However, this probably doesn't have to be the case.

A technology like FUS can most likely create clusters of experience that nature doesn't normally produce on its own. Although right now this technology is being used to explore transitions and deepening into Fundamental Wellbeing that match the current locations, this type of technology will most likely allow us to go beyond it. Possibly far beyond.

Science knows a lot about the brain. A capable brain scientist can look at the subjective, phenomenological reports for the various locations and make strongly educated guesses about which brain regions and networks are involved. At this point, much of this has been backed up by neuroimaging. All of this knowledge tells us that, in most cases, there's no reason that the changes have to cluster the way they do.

For example, it may be possible to reliably create a new location that involves the single emotion of Location 3 and the absence of agency found in Location 4, or many other combinations of the traits mentioned in this book. These are already seen on rare occasions; but they only happen for limited periods of time before Finders snap more firmly into one of the primary locations along the continuum.

Although the locations act as strong attractors, while a person's system is unstable it can temporarily exist in other, often hybrid, combinations of experiences. This happens most often when someone is new to the continuum and their system has not yet figured out which location it has the strongest affinity to. While not common, it also can happen when people are transitioning between locations. Usually in the latter case, their experience will temporarily involve a smear of their current and future location, before they fully settle into where they are heading.

Working with leaders in this area, the project has already been able to use this technology to create a hybrid form of Fundamental Wellbeing. It has been stable, and I'm personally experiencing it as I type these words. The implications of this new possibility for both Fundamental Wellbeing and humanity are profound.

For example, although there is incredible upside for anyone who currently becomes a Finder, there are often also some things it would be nice not to have to deal with, such as the changes in motivation that accompany it. A future where an optimum form of it can be, literally, engineered for each person's needs is a remarkable prospect, and would likely eliminate the aversions people currently have about why they may not want to experience it. That future is very likely already here.

APPENDIX A: HOW PEOPLE BECOME FINDERS

This book focuses on who "The Finders" are, not how to get there. This was a deliberate choice, however I know that many of you will be curious regarding what's been learned about helping people to reach Fundamental Wellbeing. It's no secret that the project has run many highly successful experiments in this area. This appendix contains a chapter excerpted from a short book I've written on this topic. If this is an area of interest for you, it can be downloaded from: **nonsymbolic.org/how-to-book**.

BECOMING A FINDER

In the core early study, roughly thirty percent of participants transitioned to Fundamental Wellbeing over time. Sometimes this process took a few hours or days, other times weeks or months. The rest experienced a shift that was immediate and sudden, like the flip of a switch.

In recent years, a Fundamental Wellbeing protocol developed by our research project called the Finders Course helped just over 70% of the hundreds of people who completed it become Finders. Surprisingly, in this research, the ways people transitioned were essentially reversed. Most transitioned over the course of a short period of time, but not instantly.

These two examples demonstrate that there probably isn't a dominant way that people become Finders. Whether you take the immediate and sudden path or transition more slowly depends on a range of factors that haven't been fully worked out yet. However, it does suggest that there is no one correct way.

WHAT TRIGGERS FUNDAMENTAL WELLBEING

The precise moment of the shift into Fundamental Wellbeing is as varied as the people who experience it. There seems to be no common subjective trigger. Finders often realize this, and can be reluctant to share the specifics of their story out of concern that others will believe it is a path to follow. This caution is understandable, but it only takes hearing a few of these accounts to realize they aren't helpful guides. In fact, it's fascinating how diverse these experiences are.

The transitions, like the Finders, reflect a cross-section of the human experience. For some, Fundamental Wellbeing arrives in moments of prayer, meditation, or contemplation. For others, it comes when they have sunk to the deepest and darkest despair of their life. Still others enter Fundamental Wellbeing during what most would consider normal day-to-day events. Examples collected during the research include, but are by no means limited to: looking out on a landscape, watching a bird land on a railing, driving down the road on the way home from work, playing with a cat, reaching for the soap during a shower, going for a walk, watching television, and getting dressed in the morning.

THE THREE WAYS OF SHIFTING INTO FUNDAMENTAL WELLBEING

The transition stories collected during the research were sorted into one of three categories. The first contained individuals who actively sought Fundamental Wellbeing. The second category was comprised of people who were depressed or in significant psychological distress at the moment of transition. The third was a catchall for those who didn't fit into either of the first two categories.

1. SEEKERS

Many Finders in the first category actively, even doggedly, pursued Fundamental Wellbeing. We'll refer to them as 'seekers.' Their range of dedication and time investment varied greatly. Some devoted the majority of their life to trying to transition. For others, it was a casual, part-time endeavor.

For those of you who want to transition, the information from these individuals may be the most important in this book. The lessons from this group suggest that the pursuit of Fundamental Wellbeing often takes far longer than is needed. Within the 'seekers' category, three paths emerged. Two seemed to lead much more rapidly to Fundamental Wellbeing than the third.

A COMMON SCENARIO

Imagine a man discovers an article about Fundamental Wellbeing, and becomes interested in it. The author mentions meditation, so this person surfs the web for more information. The more he searches, the more confused he becomes. He discovers that the internet is full of conflicting stories, techniques, and other recommendations. Eventually, he gives up and decides to start asking people he knows who have experience with it.

One friend meditates using a mantra—which she explains is simply a word or phrase repeated silently or out loud—to quiet the mind. Another describes a form of meditation he calls mindfulness. This friend says that it involves trying to pay more attention to the present moment. A third practices a form of concentration and prayer that she learned at church.

All of these friends seem excited to be asked, and rave about the difference the practices have made in their lives. After thinking it over, the person decides to try mindfulness meditation. He arrives for his lesson and discovers that it's easy to learn. He practices it together with his friend and then goes home. Over the next several days, he follows the friend's advice and tries it for an hour a day.

After a week, he has likely had one of two experiences. First, he may have felt like "something" was happening. This can range from a mind-blowing, life-altering experience to an intuitive hunch that something deeper could be going on. Alternatively, he may not have noticed anything. When he checks in, his friend encourages him to stick with it. Our research suggests that the decision made at this point is critical.

THE THREE PATHS OF THE SEEKER

Participants in the study who stuck with a technique that seemed to be doing something typically made a more rapid transition into Fundamental Wellbeing. Those willing to abandon things that were not working for them and try other techniques until they found one that produced an effect also made more rapid transitions.

Those who stuck with a practice that did not appear to be working took the longest amount of time to reach Fundamental Wellbeing, by far. Often these Finders were part of a religious or spiritual tradition that insisted it had the "best" or "only working" technique(s). These research participants typically knew others who had used the same method, and become Finders much faster. They also knew people who took even longer than they did, as well as many who hadn't made it. Often the latter category was the vast majority of people they'd known over the years who used the technique(s).

Usually their tradition had philosophical explanations for these differences that the person accepted. Examples of this included the unpredictability of God's grace, current and past life karma, and overall deservingness. These explanations were generally broad enough to cover most situations. For example, when a person transitioned to Fundamental Wellbeing more rapidly than others, but appeared less deserving, it might be attributed to the unpredictable grace of God.

TUNING WHAT'S WORKING

Many of the research participants practiced more than one technique prior to becoming a Finder. Some were part of religious or spiritual traditions that incorporated multiple methods. Others actively sought out practices that worked best for them.

These individuals generally had one or more primary technique that was working well. They paid careful attention to what it was producing, and sought out other methods when its effectiveness started to diminish. Techniques were viewed as tools. Just as a hammer isn't good for turning a screw, they viewed specific methods as relevant only for certain tasks. When it felt like one stopped working, they would assume its job was

200

done and try to find the next one that enabled progress.

Finders' use of multiple methods also showed up in another way. Some were always on the hunt for a more effective method. At any given time, these individuals had one or more techniques that were solidly working for them. However, they were continuing to experiment with variations, or new ones. These Finders not only transitioned faster than others who were pursuing Fundamental Wellbeing, they were also much more likely to shift between locations on the continuum. An important lesson here is that even if your current method is producing results, a better technique might be awaiting you.

PART-TIME OR OCCASIONAL SEEKERS

For some fortunate Finders, Fundamental Wellbeing was a casual pursuit with a rapid conclusion. These individuals are placed in the 'seeker' category, even though they put in much less effort than many of their fellow Finders. Sometimes they would transition while reading their first book about Fundamental Wellbeing. Other times, a few attempts at meditation would do the trick.

Perhaps the most common example was the Christian conversion process. A small percentage of those who "asked Jesus to come into their heart" or participated in a similar ritual immediately transitioned. Though it seemed to happen more with Christianity, the initiation rituals of other traditions also occasionally produced it. For example, a tiny number of participants transitioned during the Hindu-derived ceremony that accompanies learning Transcendental Meditation, before they ever practiced the meditation technique.

Next are those who pursued Fundamental Wellbeing, but decided to abandon their quest. These Finders are also placed in the 'seekers' category. They include individuals who tried meditation for only a brief period, sometimes years before their transition to Fundamental Wellbeing.

This also includes Finders who rigorously pursued Fundamental Wellbeing for months, years, or decades before eventually giving up. These individuals had usually thrown up their hands, convinced that nothing would ever work for them, just prior to transitioning.

Some viewed their long and dedicated spiritual practice as what was necessary to get their mind to finally accept that it had done all it could, and surrender. Others had given up their dedicated practice but were still interested in Fundamental Wellbeing and continuing to learn about it when it arrived.

2. DEPRESSION

Many Finders were not happy prior to Fundamental Wellbeing, with bouts of depression being common. Some had even attempted suicide. For clarity, the 'depression' category refers only to individuals who were both severely depressed and had never sought Fundamental Wellbeing.

Often, these individuals described themselves as being at the lowest point of their life just prior to their transition. Some, but not all, had a long history battling depression and other severe mood disorders. A tiny fraction reported the arrival of Fundamental Wellbeing during or immediately following suicide attempts. Others felt that their failed suicides were pivotal in later bringing it on.

The impact depression and suicidal thoughts can have on shifting into Fundamental Wellbeing has been known for centuries. There are even a few secretive spiritual traditions that attempt to drive their adherents to suicidal depression, in hopes it will produce the shift. Obviously, this is not a recommended path, and anyone reading this who experiences depression should seek immediate professional treatment.

After they transition, it is common for people in this category to passionately devote their lives to helping depressed individuals experience Fundamental Wellbeing. This is especially true in the years immediately following the transition. They often view it as a virtually unknown remedy that seems to work where so much else fails. Quite a few spiritual teachers in the West have this background. (Evangelical Mindfulness?)

3. THE OTHERS

This final category is a collection of individuals who transitioned without any frame of reference for Fundamental Wellbeing. They were not religious or spiritual in any way. They had not practiced any techniques relating to it, nor were they a contemplative or reflective person. They were not depressed. For them, one day the transition to Fundamental Wellbeing just happened, and they had no idea what to make of it.

The 'other' category also includes Finders who claim that a narrative sense of self never developed for them. Interviews with these individuals revealed that they had no transition story or pre-Finder history to relate. This tiny handful seems to have absolutely no idea what it is like to live with a Narrative-Self.

In some circles that study Fundamental Wellbeing, there has been considerable debate about the importance of developing, then losing, a narrative sense of self. These Finders suggest it might not be important at all. They have raised families, held down jobs, and otherwise lived outwardly 'normal' lives. During this time, it was unlikely that anyone suspected they were Finders, much less that they had never developed a Narrative-Self. They seem at least as resilient and capable as the rest of the population, and some are highly accomplished.

Again, this appendix is a chapter from a short book that we've written and are making available on this topic. The book goes into detail on the methods and structure used in our experiments that successfully transitioned just over 70% of individuals who used them to Fundamental Wellbeing, in from one week's time to four months. It covers which methods work best, how to match up to the best method for you, finding an optimum teacher or mentor, finding community, how to best avoid the "Dark Night" problem, and much more. If this is an area of interest for you, you can download it from:

nonsymbolic.org / how-to-book

APPENDIX B: DETERMINING YOUR LOCATION ON THE CONTINUUM

It's not uncommon for Finders to question whether they are, truly, on the continuum. "I seem to fit what you write here, but I'm just not sure," is a common sentiment. One of the primary reasons for this is the way human subjective experience renormalizes itself. Once a Finder, it isn't long before you genuinely cannot remember what it was like to live immersed in the Narrative-Self. While you can "sort of" think back, the accuracy of your memory diminishes over time, just as the memory of what it was like to be a 5 year-old does. You may think you remember, but in actuality you don't have any idea what it was like to actually be 'you' at that age. My best advice is: If the descriptions in this book seem to fit you, then you're a Finder. The reality is that they are very different than the way the rest of the population experiences life.

Data collection didn't stop for the first part of the study until long past the point when everyone interviewed fit into one of the locations, except for those in the furthest locations, who continue to trickle in over time. Despite this, it can be difficult for some Finders to determine their location on the continuum. The major reason for this is simple: what Finders focus on most naturally in their moment to moment experience is not what the project uses to evaluate them.

The research is centered on cognitive science questions involving: the sense of self, cognition, affect, perception, and memory. As mentioned previously, these are what allowed the research to successfully traverse so many populations for, as far as is known, the first time in history. Virtually no one had considered their experience of Fundamental Wellbeing through these lenses, which is one reason the interviews lasted so long. Even teachers who had diligently answered questions from many thousands of students, or more, over decades typically had to take time and reflect before answering.

The questions they'd spent so many years responding to were typically ones that seemed more salient to those doing the asking. Here are just a couple examples, out of probably billions: "I've recently had a shift. What has felt for some time like an empty void infused by love now feels like love infused in the world in a very peculiar way. What do you make of that?" "There is no me, but at the same time I feel so completely embodied, what is going on?" These types of questions are, obviously, very different than the kind the project asked.

Spaciousness, consciousness, emptiness, no doer, love, compassion, and many other similar topics have traditionally been dominant themes for those within Fundamental Wellbeing. Early on, when the project was dealing with distinguished teachers from a major Buddhist tradition, it became clear that none of them agreed with each other on the specifics of the path of their tradition. Each had the same names for the stages, and so forth; however when asked for the phenomenological markers associated with a given stage the answers were not only different, but often conflicting. When the project inquired about the discrepancies, the teacher being asked would most commonly say that the others were well meaning, but just didn't really get it.

This is one reason why it can be a good idea for both seekers and Finders to search out the tradition, institution, or person who best fits them. Probably the most agreed upon sets of experience are within the Islamic and Christian mystical traditions. This seems to relate to the strength of their central dogma and also the limited number of locations they focus on. However, even within these traditions, it's a good idea to shop around, so to speak. One Finder mentioned going to literally dozens of churches, month after month, during his seeking before he found the one where "God revealed himself."

Given that the leaders within a tradition often can't agree, it's not surprising that there is so much disagreement across traditions. The same is seen within the academic world where there are intense philosophical debates about all of this. For example, the common core faction argues that people's experiences as Finders largely boil down to a central set of related experiences. The constructivist faction argues that there is no common core, and that many factors, such as culture, combine to give people experiences that may or may not be similar to each other. The participatory faction has a "many shores" around a central lake type of view that also attempts to explain why people seem to have such varied yet similar experiences.

In the project's data, if you dig deep enough, all of these make sense. The closer to the surface of someone's psychology you go, the more the constructivist and participatory views seem to be the case. However, when one goes down far enough using the latest tools science has to offer, support for the common core emerges. In our work, this is all reflected in the continuum.

A Finder's internal world is rarely, if ever, focused by default on the aspects of cognitive science that our project utilized. It's much more likely to be directed to its dominant internal experiences, which can include things like spaciousness and the other items mentioned previously. This makes it easy to understand why so many pages have been filled by Finders on those types of topics. It comes naturally.

It's much easier than a Finder trying to force him or herself to view things through our more scientifically objectified lens. For this reason, a certain percentage always give up and just say that they don't feel there is a location that really fits them. So far, each time one of these individuals has sat for a full-length research interview, their perspective has changed. However, it can take this level of effort to really figure it out.

To sort themselves on the continuum, Finders must commit themselves to looking at their internal experiences through the lenses the research project used. Obviously, there's no substitute for an expert research interviewer sitting with you, and helping you to probe your inner experience for six to twelve hours. However, it is still possible to get a sense of where you are without going to that extreme. Many find that they can do it by just reading the descriptions in this book. Some of our research subjects created elaborate spreadsheets based on what is mentioned here to more thoroughly evaluate themselves.

While that can probably be helpful, it's rarely necessary. For those who have difficulty, it can be useful to just consider one aspect at a time, and ask questions relating to that. Below is a simple sequence of questions that can be used to get started, and that might be helpful if you think you could be a Finder but are having difficulty placing yourself. Just note which answer you most resonate with for each question. A scoring key follows at the end. Keep in mind, that this short series of questions is by no means comprehensive or definitive. Unless you are very clearly in Location 4, you probably won't be able to determine your location just from the questions that follow. It's only presented here to help you get started in how to think about situating yourself on the continuum.

QUESTIONS

Q1. Which of the following statements is most true about your emotions...

    a. I don't experience emotion for the most part or at all.

    b. I primarily experience a simple emotional life that feels like one unified emotion that is combination of things such as divine or impersonal love, joy, and compassion.

    c. I experience a mix of positive and negative emotions, but it is mostly positive and negative emotions that usually disappear almost as quickly as they appear.

    d. I experience a mix of positive and negative emotions, but negative emotions usually disappear almost as quickly as they appear.

    e. I experience a mix of positive and negative emotions.

Q2. Which of the following statements is most true about your thoughts and thinking...

    a. At some point in my life, I experienced a change where my mind became mostly or entirely quiet; I experience very few thoughts or none at all.

    b. At some point in my life, I experienced a change where my mind was suddenly full of many more thoughts, but they don't seem to be able to affect me emotionally.

    c. It often seems like there is a "voice" in my head that is offering opinions about things and affecting my emotions.

    d. It sometimes seems like there is a "voice" in my head that is offering opinions about things but it does not affect my emotions.

Q3. Which of the following statements is most true about your visual perception…

    a. When I see the world, I experience it as everything just showing up all at once; it doesn't feel as if I'm looking out at it.

    b. When I see the world, it feels like I, or at least something that seems like me, is looking out at it through my eyes or from behind my eyes.

Q4. Which of the following statements is most true about your auditory perception…

    a. When I listen to the world, I experience all of the sounds from the current moment just showing up at once.

    b. When I listen to the world, it feels like I, or at least something that seems like me, is listening out from my ears, or from inside my head out through my ears.

Q5. Which of the following statements is most true about your memories…

    a. I'm concerned that my memory isn't working well; memories rarely pop up and I don't think I remember my life events very well.

    b. Memories seem to pop up less than they used to; they just don't seem to come to mind like they once did.

    c. My memory seems pretty normal for my age; I seem to remember things about as well as others my age do.

Q6. Which of the following statement is most true…

    a. I am able to make choices and decisions, take actions, and so on.

    b. Actions, choices, and decisions happen, but I don't feel like I am necessarily doing them. It does seem like there are 'correct' choices in most or every situation.

    c. I am not able to make any choices or decisions, or take any actions, although things seem to keep unfolding and happening anyway.

ANSWER KEY

Q1: **a.** L4 or later; **b.** L3; **c.** L1 or L2, **d.** L1, **e.** nNSE

Q2: **a.** L1, 2, 3, 4, or later; b. L1 or 2; c. - nNSE; **d.** nNSE or L1

Q3: **a.** L2 or L4, or later; **b.** nNSE

Q4: **a.** L2 or L4, or later; **b.** nNSE

Q5: **a.** L2, L3, L4, or later; **b.** L1, L2, or L3; **c.** nNSE, L1, L2, or L3

Q6 **a.** nNSE or L1; **b.** L2; c. L4

APPENDIX C: MENTAL ILLNESS OR FUNDAMENTAL WELLBEING?

I don't want this book to imply that the research never encounters individuals with mental illness who also purport to experience Fundamental Wellbeing. Individuals with strong forms of bi-polar, mania, and psychosis, for example, can make claims involving the experience of states that sound like they might be far-out locations on the continuum. However, it is important to note that this is a tiny minority of individuals who are potentially claiming to be Finders. And, it does sometimes seem to be the case that temporary forms of these experiences can leave Fundamental Wellbeing in their wake.

This is one of the most difficult areas within this topic of research. It seems unquestionable that mental illness is involved. These individuals are often institutionalized and medicated before their condition improves. It's equally unquestionable that some of their experiences seem to match descriptions that relate to aspects of Fundamental Wellbeing. In fact, it can be very hard to determine where pathology leaves off and Fundamental Wellbeing might begin.

Generally, the view within the project is that these types of experiences are best related to and treated as mental illness. Over the years we have come across several individuals and clinics that strongly believe otherwise. These attempt to assist people who have serious bi-polar, manic, or psychotic episodes in using their experiences to transition to Fundamental Wellbeing. To date we have not seen results from these efforts that suggest they are advisable. People who utilize them often go off their medications and become re-institutionalized.

Perhaps not surprisingly, the individuals who lead these types of efforts typically had the same types of experience, but genuinely feel that they led to Fundamental Wellbeing. In their cases, that certainly might be true. However, the project has encountered so many people who failed in these types of attempts that, at least as of this writing, this is not something we feel is a good idea to try.

Having said that, an opportunity may exist to enter Fundamental Wellbeing once the episode has ended, or the mental illness has been tamed by medications. Some of the core aspects of Fundamental Wellbeing, such as deep peace, a quiet mind, and so forth can be present at that time. Focus on these has successfully led quite a number of individuals to Fundamental Wellbeing, just as can be the case after someone has a peak experience (see Chapter 25). When pharmaceuticals are prescribed it is typical to dislike them, because experiences like mania can be so compelling. We have not seen evidence that they block or prevent the experience of Fundamental Wellbeing.

APPENDIX D: A VERY BRIEF LOOK AT SOME DATA

The research project has generated a massive amount of data on Fundamental Wellbeing over the last 12 years. It seems appropriate to include a small taste of it for those of you who are interested in it. A great deal more is available on the center's website (**nonsymbolic.org**).

Since 2014 the project has been running a first-of-its-kind experiment known as the Finders Course to collect psychological and physiological data on people before and after their transition to Fundamental Wellbeing. As this book goes to press, the data from eleven Finders Course experiments have been analyzed. Four hundred and fifty-five participants successfully completed the program out of five hundred and seventy-one who began, approximately an 80% completion rate.

Of these, three hundred and nineteen (or an incredible 70%) of those who completed it reported a transition to Fundamental Wellbeing. And, a majority of the remaining participants reported at least temporary glimpses of Fundamental Wellbeing during the program.

At this point the program has included people from six continents and dozens of countries, including many who speak English as a second language. Ages have ranged from twenty-one to eighty-one. People came from a wide variety of backgrounds and professions. A broad range of gold standard psychology measures was used to collect data from each cohort, including the following:

- *CES-D: Center for Epidemiological Studies Depression Scale*
- *PERMA: Positive emotion, Engagement, Relationships, Meaning, Accomplishment*
- *FEQ: Fordyce Emotions Questionnaire*
- *PSS: Perceived Stress Scale*
- *NEO-FFI: Neuroticism-Extraversion-Openness Five-Factor Inventory*

- *CRQ: Close Relationships Questionnaire*
- *STAI-Y2: State-Trait Anxiety Inventory (Trait Anxiety)*
- *SWLS: Satisfaction with Life Scale*
- *GHS: General Happiness Scale*

The table below shows the percentage change for participants who completed the program for several of the major measures. Some measures were rotated in and out over time, so not all measures were given to each participant. If you're familiar with these measures from other research, the changes will seem huge to you. They are.

Overall the program has a massive impact on participant wellbeing. Also note the large drop in the personality trait Neuroticism. Personality traits are supposed to be relatively durable over time, so a drop like this over a four-month program is remarkable. Importantly, all changes are highly statically significant ($p < 0.00001$).

Percentage of change for participants from beginning of Finder's Course to completion

Measure	Percent Change
Depression (CES-D)	-47%
Loneliness (PERMA)	-46%
Percent of Time Unhappy (FEQ)	-46%
Negative Affect (PERMA)	-41%
Stress (PSS)	-34%
Neuroticism (NEO-FFI)	-32%
Attachment-Related Anxiety (CRQ)	-26%
Persistent Anxiety (STAI Y-2)	-21%
Percent of Time Happy (FEQ)	+35%
Satisfaction with Life (SWLS)	+21%
Positive Emotion (PERMA)	+20%
General Happiness Scale (GHS)	+20%

Another way to look at the data is to ask if there is a difference between participants who reported a transition to Fundamental Wellbeing (FW) or not by the end of the program. The no Fundamental Wellbeing, or nFW, category includes both those who experienced temporary Fundamental Wellbeing as well as no glimpses of Fundamental Wellbeing at all. Recall that most people in this category would have experienced at least some glimpses of Fundamental Wellbeing.

Longitudinal research, including at least one project that spanned decades, have shown that glimpses of Fundamental Wellbeing are often regarded by people as among the most transformative and significant experiences of their lives. In fact, we do see quite remarkable improvements in the nFW group. However, it is not nearly as profound as changes experienced by those reporting Fundamental Wellbeing.

If a glimpse was as transformative as a full transition to Fundamental Wellbeing, we'd expect to see the two groups being close together in their numbers. In fact, they are quite far apart. It's very clear that the group that experiences Fundamental Wellbeing is in a very different place in terms of their experience of the world than the group that does not. Importantly, the difference between the groups on every measure is highly statically significant ($p < 0.00001$).

The "% Difference" column in the next table might seem confusing to you. It is calculated on the difference between the ending score for each group. So, for example, let's say the total score for a happiness measure was between 0 (miserable) and 100 (gloriously happy). If the FW group's final score was 100, and the nFW group's final score was 50, the FW group would be 100% happier than the nFW group. You can see a lot more about these types of changes on our academic website, in some of my detailed presentations.

Comparing percentage change for participants at the end of the course who reported being in Fundamental Wellbeing (FW) with participants who did not report Fundamental Wellbeing (nFW)

Measure	% Change FW	% Change nFW	% Difference
Depression (CES-D)	-60%	-25%	-60%
Loneliness (PERMA)	-58%	-27%	-56%
Percent Time Unhappy (FEQ)	-56%	-29%	-56%
Negative Affect (PERMA)	-51%	-25%	-49%
Stress (PSS)	-41%	-19%	-41%
Neuroticism (NEO-FFI)	-39%	-18%	-43%
Anxiety (STAI Y-2)	-25%	-14%	-26%
Percent Time Happy (FEQ)	+37%	+30%	+41%
Satisfaction with Life (SWLS)	+24%	+14%	+27%
Positive Emotion (PERMA)	+21%	+16%	+25%
General Happiness (GHS)	+22%	+15%	+25%

In addition to using gold-standard psychology questionnaires, participants were also asked some general questions, such as if they had more inner peace after the program. The results from some of those questions are in the table below. These numbers are not the amount of increase, just the number of people that reported more or less of a given experience as a result of the course.

Top Percentage categories for all participants who completed course

Question	More	Question	Less
Inner Peace	88%	Reactivity	83%
Mindfulness	83%	Negative Thoughts	82%
Gratitude	82%	Negative Emotions	81%
Happiness	80%	Anxiety	77%
Emotional Balance	79%		
Contentedness	78%		
Positive Emotions	78%		

The two tables below compare the scores for participants who reported transitioning into Fundamental Wellbeing versus those who did not. Although most categories are the same, notice that the lowest score in the FW list is well above the highest score in the nFW list. Also notice the categories that are different. The FW list includes two categories that the nFW list does not: Emotional Balance and Contentedness. Conversely, the nFW list also has two unique categories: Gratitude and Tolerance of Others.

Consider the difference between these four items. Two of them are nearly impossible to will yourself to control: Emotional Balance and Contentedness. Although many people try to force states like these to occur, ultimately these just happen. They really cannot be willed or forced to occur without causing their opposite.

Now consider the other two items from the nFW list: Gratitude and Tolerance of Others. While wonderful attributes, these can be forced. You can sit down right now and make yourself feel gratitude, for instance. Of course, these can also naturally arise, but in many ways these two items highlight a key difference in Fundamental Wellbeing.

The traits that comprise the psychological experience of Fundamental Wellbeing often just arise with no additional action needed. It is literally a new norm that appears in one's experience, not something that has to be actively maintained in each moment.

Another thing to note in the tables below is that, even for the highest category in the nFW list, the Fundamental Wellbeing group has a higher reported percentage. In other words, participants reporting Fundamental Wellbeing at the end of the course also reported higher levels of both Gratitude and Tolerance of Others. Also, notice how rapidly the top scores for the no Fundamental Wellbeing group drop off compared to the participants who reported Fundamental Wellbeing.

Top 5 percentage categories where 'more is better' for participants who completed course that reported Fundamental Wellbeing (FW) vs. no Fundamental Wellbeing (nFW)

Question	FW	nFW
Inner Peace	92%	79%
Emotional Balance	88%	58%
Mindfulness	88%	72%
Happiness	87%	62%
Contentedness	87%	58%

Top 5 percentage categories where 'more is better' for participants who completed course that reported no Fundamental Wellbeing (nFW) vs. Fundamental Wellbeing (FW)

Question	FW	nFW
Inner Peace	92%	79%
Gratitude	86%	72%
Mindfulness	88%	72%
Tolerance of Others	85%	64%
Happiness	87%	62%

What about items that are ideal to have go down, like negative thoughts and emotions? Here again we see key differences between the two groups, and our previous observations hold up. The lowest score for the Fundamental Wellbeing group is still above the highest score for those who didn't report experiencing it, there are huge differences in the percentage reporting being in the various categories between the two groups, and so on.

All of the categories are shared between the groups, except for two. A large reduction is reported in internal mental chatter in the Fundamental

Wellbeing group but not in the no Fundamental Wellbeing group. As outlined in this book and many of our other materials, the reduction of internal narrative is a key component of Fundamental Wellbeing. The other difference is a reduction in conflict that shows up as one of the categories for those who do not experience Fundamental Wellbeing, though at a far lower level than for those who do.

Top 5 percentage categories where 'less is better' for participants who completed course that reported Fundamental Wellbeing (FW) vs. no Fundamental Wellbeing (nFW)

Question	FW	nFW
Fewer Negative Thoughts	90%	63%
Less Reactivity	88%	71%
Fewer Negative Emotions	88%	64%
Less Mental Internal Chatter	85%	52%
Less Anxiety	85%	61%

Top 5 percentage categories where 'less is better' for participants who completed course that reported no Fundamental Wellbeing (nFW) vs. Fundamental Wellbeing (FW)

Question	FW	nFW
Less Reactivity	88%	71%
Fewer Negative Emotions	88%	64%
Fewer Negative Thoughts	90%	63%
Less Conflict	83%	61%
Less Anxiety	85%	61%

We were fortunate to have this project be the first in modern history that could reliably, safely and rapidly produce a transition in such a high percentage of people into Fundamental Wellbeing, and thus allow tracking the before and after changes. No matter how this data is examined, it is clear that these are two groups of people who are experiencing the world through very different internal lenses. Both groups improved significantly across major scientific measures of wellbeing, emotion, personality, and more. In fact, if the experimental protocol had only produced the changes seen in the group that did not report Fundamental Wellbeing, it would have been a smashing success.

As incredible as the changes for all participants were, the results reported by Finders across the entire spectrum were significantly and measurably higher. It's completely clear which group you'd want to be in, given the opportunity. The good news is that you can be!

This appendix is based on a chapter from the short book mentioned previously. The book goes into detail on the methods and structure used in our experiments that successfully transitioned just over 70% of individuals who used them to Fundamental Wellbeing, in from one week's time to four months. It covers which methods work best, how to match up to the best method for you, finding an optimum teacher or mentor, finding community, how to best avoid the "Dark Night" problem, and much more. If this is an area of interest for you, you can download it from: **nonsymbolic.org/how-to-book**.

APPENDIX E: FURTHER RESOURCES

RESEARCH PROJECT AND STUDY INFORMATION

The Center for the Study of Non-Symbolic Consciousness conducted the research that forms the backbone of this book. The publication page of its website contains a wide variety of presentations, interviews, reports, articles, and more. If you experience Fundamental Wellbeing or are a scientist wanting to research it, you can also sign up on the site to participate in research projects. The Center's website can be found at:

NonSymbolic.org

FOR SEEKERS

The experiment that has traditionally helped just over 70% of people who participate in it transition to Fundamental Wellbeing is the Finders Course. This experiment is the first large-scale, crowd-sourced, crowd-funded international research project targeted at helping participants shift into Fundamental Wellbeing, and the rest of the world learn about this important change that can occur within human psychology. It's not too late to participate. It can be found at:

FindersCourse.com

FOR FINDERS

As you may recall from the book, one way to visualize the path to and through Fundamental Wellbeing is people shifting from seekers to Finders, and from Finders to Explorers. Because of the number of people who have transitioned to Fundamental Wellbeing during the Finders Course, a follow-up research sub-project and accompanying experiment, called the Explorers Course, was created. This project is designed to help Finders optimally integrate and grow into Fundamental Wellbeing, regardless of whether they transitioned or decades ago. It's based on best practices from around the world that were learned during the research. You can find it at:

ExplorersCourse.com

ABOUT THE AUTHOR

Jeffery A. Martin, PhD, is a scientist, technologist, entrepreneur, and investor who focuses on advancing the highest forms of human wellbeing. For over a decade he has conducted the largest international study into ongoing and persistent forms of non-symbolic experience (ONE/PNSE), which includes the types of consciousness commonly known as: enlightenment, nonduality, the peace that passeth understanding, unitive experience, and hundreds of other terms. This book refers to these as *Fundamental Wellbeing*. His research resulted in the first reliable, cross-cultural and pan-tradition classification system for these types of experience. More recently, he has used this research to make protocols and information available that help people obtain profound psychological benefits in a rapid, secular, reliable, and safe way.

Dr. Martin is also the founder of the Transformative Technology ecosystem, which promotes the use of science and technology to substantially raise human mental and emotional wellbeing. Since he conceived of and created the space in 2007, he has been a catalyst in bringing together makers, scientists and other researchers, engineers, entrepreneurs, companies, educational institutions, non-profits and NGO's, public policy experts, and investors. He co-founded the first academic TransTech lab, its first conference, taught the first university-level course, organized the first investor gatherings, and many other firsts. He serves as a formal and informal advisor to a wide range of companies and other organizations in the space, is an active early-stage investor, and is a frequent public speaker on Transformative Technology related topics.

In addition to his wellbeing work, Dr. Martin is a bestselling author and award-winning educator who has authored, co-authored, or co-edited over twenty books. His work has regularly been featured at leading academic conferences worldwide, as well as major public forums such as Wisdom 2.0, H+, the Science and Nonduality Conference, the Asia Consciousness Festival, Deepak Chopra's Sages and Scientists Symposium, and TEDx. He has been covered in media as diverse as the South China Morning Post and PBS's Closer to Truth, and been an invited speaker at many top universities including: Harvard, Yale, Stanford, University of London, and the National University of Singapore.

Among other roles, he is currently the Director of the Center for the Study of Non-Symbolic Consciousness, a Research Professor and Director at the Transformative Technology Lab in Silicon Valley, and co-founder of Alchemas, Inc., which is pioneering the use of brain stimulation for Fundamental Wellbeing. Dr. Martin has served on the faculty of several universities, including as a visiting professor in the School of Design at Hong Kong Polytechnic University, and as a Distinguished University Professor, the William James Professor of Consciousness Studies, and Dean of Research at Sofia University. His personal website is: **DrJefferyMartin.com**